Storytellers' True Stories About Love

Volume 2

Edited by

Judi Lee Goshen & Anne E. Beall

Chicago Story Press, Inc.

CHICAGO STORY PRESS

STORYTELLERS' TRUE STORIES ABOUT LOVE
VOLUME 2

Cover Designed by Atiq Ahmed with image licensed through 123rf.com

ISBN: 97989874649-0-8 (Paperback)
ISBN: 97989874649-1-5 (Hard Cover)

Table of Contents

Introduction

We can only learn to love by loving.
~Iris Murdoch

With such a warm and encouraging response to our last book, *Storytellers' True Stories About Love*, we felt compelled to publish a second volume. The theme seems to speak to writers; they recall first loves, lost loves, animals, family members, and that crazy time when they ignored all reason and did the impossible.

We had almost 100 submissions, and although we wish we could have published them all, we selected thirty true stories that spoke about how love plays a role at every stage of life. The stories are poignant, funny, thought-provoking, and relatable. They caused us to cry, laugh out loud, and ultimately feel better about the world we inhabit.

Our lives are full of short stories. These tales tell where we've been, what we want, and what has influenced us. Although everyone's stories may be similar in theme, they are as varied and as personal as our own DNA. And when storytellers share their stories, we feel validated and less alone in our unique experiences. This book reflects the love that occurs throughout life, and how it transforms us at every stage.

The first encounters with love occur in our family. The people who cared for us, raised us, and who taught us about what it means to love. So, it is no surprise there are several stories about mothers. One heroic mother overcomes a mental illness long enough to teach her son a valuable tool, a gift that not only helps him through school, but ends up setting him on a career path. Another mother sacrifices her own needs, moving into a substandard part of their home to give her teenage daughter a room to call her own.

Parents love children even before they come into this world. One father writes about the difficulties of conception and the love he feels for a child long before it is born. And the mother of adopted children shows us the mothering is a verb, it's love in action regardless of a biological connection.

Siblings are another source of love and inspiration. Although these relationships can be challenging, their influence is profound. One author shows how her siblings enable her to climb to great heights because they see past her disability. Another author's love for his older brother and deep desire to communicate with him helps his brother and an entire deaf community.

When it's difficult to feel love from the people in your household, a grandparent can step in. This avenue of love can give children the validation they desperately need. One grandmother gives the gift of a college education so her granddaughter can pursue her dreams, while another provides a safe haven when her granddaughter needs a break from a dysfunctional family. Both gifts instill a foundation of love and support that is so important.

Outside the family, teachers and other important people can bestow love in ways that reverberate for years. A teacher who takes an interest in a broken child leads her to pursue a unique career and to approach her profession in a way that makes her students feel loved and safe. The legacy of this one educator affects many lives.

Storytellers also explore young romantic love, which is complicated. Our first crushes can have overwhelming and intense feelings, as one author describes when a boy cannot reciprocate her love. Another writer remembers fondly the sweet, troubled boys in the hood she left behind and the myriad feelings she has for them as she looks back on that time.

The love we have for our pets and their unconditional love for us also form our understanding about love. These creatures teach us patience, perseverance, and friendship. One author shares a story about her first love, a horse named Dandy, who shows her what it means to truly connect with another being and what caring means in difficult circumstances. Another shares her rescue of a newborn duckling, and although the duckling is not a pet, she returns every spring. Relationships with animals involve some level of vulnerability with one's heart that is repaid in spades.

Love often finds you when you least expect it, and sometimes when you just want to get out of the rain. One author describes how the need for an umbrella leads her to the love of her life. Many authors describe how they didn't expect to fall in love and were fine with their lives until someone disrupted their routines. Apparently, one cannot plan for love.

Love connections are powerful and lead us to do impossible things. One author rescues her boyfriend from nearly drowning and wonders how she scaled a high cliff to do so. She's still wondering. Another author writes about fostering a troubled youth and how that love helps her heal her own wounds and open her heart to a different life.

Love can be difficult, particularly when a romantic relationship must overcome cultural differences, personality issues, and the realities of modern life. Although many storytellers tell us about finding that special someone, it isn't always possible to stay with that person for reasons that are out of their control. The lessons they learn are valuable. One author recounts how his girlfriend's family will not accept him because of his religion and another writer describes how the things that drew him to his boyfriend are also what causes their disintegration as a couple.

As we become adults, looking back at the one who got away through mature eyes may have us wondering what might have been. Two of our authors write about revisiting past loves to see if there might be a future with this person. Their journeys yield surprising, different outcomes.

Love changes along with our views of romantic relationships. One writer describes how the communication with her husband changes from the witty verbal exchanges she values in their youth to silent moments of contentment. Moments she now treasures, but once avoided because she was concerned that silence indicated a relationship breakdown.

Although the love for another is important, love for oneself is essential. During a difficult time when she could have retreated into isolation, one author builds herself up by creating a new life and giving herself many new experiences that lead to greater self-love. Another author describes how she escapes the self-loathing of seeing her estranged father's features in the mirror when she realizes they are the features of her loving grandmother.

When the cycle of life claims a loved one, they may be gone, but the emotion and its effect still lives on. One author, while caring for her dying mother, takes an improv class to get out of her head, and learns to be in the moment with her mother during the most heart-wrenching times. It ends up being the best gift for both her and her dying mother. After the passing of the family matriarch, one author recounts how the extended family finds their new normal and eventually honors their lost family member.

When a loved one is no longer in this world, their strong presence remains. For example, one woman describes how she opened a portal of communication with her father as he left this world, and another storyteller describes how she sees communication beyond the grave in the most unusual places. Another author feels her mother coming to her through the stories that people share about her mom.

The stories in this book teach us how we learn to love, the risks we take to keep it, how it inspires, and how it never disappears. We hope this book will bring joy and inspiration to you.

Judi Lee Goshen & Anne E. Beall

1 | Fifty-Six Ways to Say I Love Me by Beth Holly

Is there anything better than the beginning of something? The anticipation of the first pitch when the game belongs to anyone. The smell of dough rising. The dimming of the theater lights. The first kiss. Oh, the first delicious kiss, tasting of possibility.

It had been a long time since I had savored the pleasure of a new beginning. My marriage had been on life-support for longer than was merciful, and I finally freed myself. Too many of my best parts had shriveled on arid soil during my marriage, and I longed to replenish them. To breathe life once again into the joy and wonder I had lost. My ex-husband's narrow comfort zone had confined my world, and my dreams of exotic travel and daring adventure had given way to repeat visits to Vermont in the winter, Cape Cod in the summer. For far too long. Now, with only myself to consult, my horizons had blown wide open.

Longing for novelty, I took my first trip just a few months after leaving my marriage. Dear friends were celebrating thirty years of marriage with a renewal of vows on the island of Oahu that coincided with my fifty-sixth birthday. While celebrating a vow renewal just as I had revoked my own carried more than a hint of irony, I relished the opportunity to travel and be among their big, crazy family on my first birthday as a reimagined single. This was my first trip to Hawaii and to make the most of it, I had signed up for a weeklong surf and yoga retreat on Maui following the event. I was neither a surfer nor a yogi. Just a reborn woman looking for adventure.

Having never set foot on a surfboard, a preliminary lesson before joining the program seemed sensible. The vow renewal wasn't until evening, so early on my birthday morning I made my way to the hotel surf shop for a lesson. As I rifled through a basket of fermented loaner rash guards, those skin-tight shirts that make surfers look buff, a shirtless Jeff Spicoli look-alike ambled my way.

"Hey. You're here for a surf lesson? Awesome. I'm Chase."

I didn't know whether to swoon or laugh, but Chase was picture perfect for my Hawaiian adventure. I grabbed the least smelly rash guard and followed Chase into a bright pink minibus. Feeling like a kid on a school trip, I pressed my nose against the window to capture as much Hawaiian majesty as possible. We wove among jagged mountains covered in a carpet of green. Extraordinary tropical flowers grew like weeds at the side of the road. Pods of surfers floated on deep blue water waiting for the next big swell.

I suddenly remembered those surfing videos on YouTube that I'd tagged but never watched. I was in the best physical shape of my life, but all I knew about surfing I learned watching the film, *Point Break*. We pulled into the parking lot of a small surf break and Chase grabbed our boards as we made our way onto the beach. I was relieved to see that we'd be starting on the sand, and I had no trouble bouncing up into an empowering warrior pose. Having gotten a few pop-ups under my belt, I felt confident as we paddled out into what looked like gentle surf.

Gentle was an illusion. Turns out popping up is a lot harder when the surfboard is moving under your feet. Time and time again I hit the surf, trying in vain to ride atop, instead of beneath the waves. Chase did an admirable job trying to keep my body and spirits up, and after seven or eight face plants, I stood on the board for a nanosecond or two and declared victory. Floating astride my board with a grin as big as my sense of accomplishment, I thanked Chase for making my fifty-sixth birthday memorable.

"That's so rad that you went surfing for the first time on your birthday," said Chase as we slowly paddled our way back to shore, the unspoken "at your age" hanging in the salty air. "You're like my grandma. She just turned seventy, and she said she's going to do seventy new things this year."

I didn't care that I'd just been compared to a grandma. I was rad.

Chase's grandma surfed her way through my thoughts all day. I loved the idea of committing to do fifty-six new things in the year to come, and as the Hawaiian sun set in a blaze of glorious color, I made her pledge my own. I didn't know what the new things would be. I made no bucket list. I chose only to be open to possibility. To welcome adventure and novelty into a life that had too long been stuck in painful repetition. To give my eyes the gift of unseen places and my tongue the delight of new flavors. To challenge my body and sharpen my mind. To embrace the universe and feel its embrace in return.

Surfing became number one on what would become a list of fifty-six new things accomplished over the course of a year. Over the months that followed, I populated the list with exotic new foods—duck feet in Shanghai and mofongo in Puerto Rico—and common ones that had somehow escaped my palate, like the not-to-be-repeated pimento olive. I traveled to places I'd never been, sometimes solo, sometimes with friends, always with eyes and grin wide open. I jumped off a waterfall, rode in the back of a pickup truck, and shot a handgun—all because I'd never done those things before. With mindful gratitude for every opportunity, I embraced the gifts the universe bestowed.

Diving into the dating pool, I found an ample opportunity for firsts. Online dating, one-night stands, kinky encounters, all found a place on my list of fifty-six things. I played my first round of golf and traded my skis for a snowboard, reminding myself what it felt like to be a beginner. I did things alone I had always done in pairs, like going to a concert and buying a house, proving to myself repeatedly that I could. Each new adventure infused my undernourished soul, making "hell yes!" my new mantra. I had no boundaries. If it was new, I was in, and I was insatiable.

Enter Covid.

Travel came screeching to a halt, as did dating, concerts and so many potential firsts. My world got smaller, as did my opportunities to do new things. Wiping down my groceries for the first time wasn't exactly scratching my itch. But as this was going to be more than a two-week hiatus from the office, I redefined my expectations for new things. Instead of trekking through Nepal, I learned how to sew facemasks. Instead of skydiving, I joined a Black Lives Matter rally. I attended a joyful backyard movie and a heartbreaking Zoom funeral. I created a TikTok account to chronical my fifty-six things (it's number forty-seven on the list) and found an audience eager to hear about my journey from unhappy marriage to joy.

Change arrives without notice or invitation, as reliable as the morning sun, creating daily the opportunity for a new beginning. The pandemic hibernation, which at first seemed limiting, proved fertile ground for growth. It didn't matter I was learning to cut my hair instead of seeing foreign lands. I was learning, growing, and thriving. Relieved of the burden of an unhappy marriage, I became a living constellation of beginnings, forever seeking the new. Like the moonflower that waits for the night to reveal its silky, white blooms, I blossomed in the pandemic darkness.

As the New York sun set in glorious color over the Hudson River, I capped my list of fifty-six things by blowing out my birthday candles with my hands. Surrounded by friends who scaffolded me through the hard times and welcomed me in the new, I celebrated the unexpected joy of 2020. For amid the darkness that enveloped our globe, I found light. I chose to expand rather than contract. With each new entry on my list, I grew more confident, more centered, more radiant. I gave myself fifty-six birthday presents, fifty-six opportunities to grow, fifty-six expressions of love. For I am the first pitch, the rising dough, the dimming lights. I am the intoxicating first kiss.

***

Beth Holly is in the midst of a personal renaissance, having recently ended a twenty-eight-year marriage and a thirty-five-year legal career. Writing has become the vehicle for speaking the truth of her experience and sharing her rediscovered thirst for adventure, learning, and joy. Working in memoir, fiction and poetry, Beth's writing is raw and brave and bridges from the deeply personal to the universal. Her work has been published in *HerStry* and *Grande Dame Literary Journal*. Find out more at www.bethholly.com.

2 | My Mother the Pro by Sean Ewert

I am thirteen years old—sweaty, stinky, and with huge curly hair.

I know what it's like not to have a friend in the world. We move a lot because of my mother's mental illness. My mother's obsessive-compulsive disorder (OCD) and the many voices in her head always tell her when it is time to run. I attend five elementary schools. On one occasion, I only stay for a month. I am good at being the new kid. But nobody really knows me or my mother's secret, which we both carry.

The moves catch up with me and I end up friendless in seventh grade.

My junior high is a brutalist soviet era looking building with no windows, it literally looks like a prison. My teachers are incredibly strange. Mr. Smith stands on his desk and delivers his English class lectures and Ms. Michaels, the reading teacher, slinks around her carpeted classroom like a cat. It's like a huge scratching post to her. No one will talk to me. I eat lunch alone and read *Motor Trend* magazine in the library. The other kids can tell that I am different.

To make friends, I decide to audition for a musical. Dressed in my finest baby blue Izod polo and Levi's 501 jeans, I feel good as I approach the school auditorium. I wait, pacing back and forth in my Sperry Topsiders. My name is called. I walk to my spot. The piano starts. I sing *Happy Birthday*.

Then, silence.

From where I'm standing, I can only see a tight bun of grey hair. Finally, the lady says, "You can't sing. You'll never be able to sing."

Defeated, I go home.

Luckily for me, they don't have enough males. The wall phone in the kitchen rings later that night. I have the part; I will play the

King in *The Princess and the Magic Pea* and sing a song. The problem is, I've never been in a play before, and I don't know how to sing. And my voice is changing daily.

I consider asking my mother for some help. However, we have made a very grown-up agreement when I was in the first grade that I would be responsible for my homework. She made it clear her mental illness would not let her help me.

I approach her anyway. I am desperate.

Like a Hollywood agent deciding whether to take a new actor on, my mother mulls over my casting situation. She evaluates me across the kitchen table. She adjusts the pale pink fuzzy bathrobe she never takes off. My mother sighs and paces, twisting her long black hair. She looks through her piles of paper as if she is checking her calendar.

"Fine," she says. "I'll do it."

"Do what?" I ask.

"I'll coach you," she replies.

"How?"

"I'll teach you how to sing and act. I know what I'm doing."

"I'm scared to go onstage. What if I forget my lines or nothing comes out of me?" I ask.

She says, "It's part of performing. It can all fall apart. That's the risk. You could be bad. It's not a reason not to try. More often, you'll be good, I assure you." Then my mother takes my hands, looks me straight in the eye and asks, "Can I please do this for you? It's the only thing I have to give you."

I am totally taken by surprise. This feeling. She wants to help me. I feel for the first time what it is like to have my mother engaged in my life. I'm so giddy. This is love.

"Yes, please help me," I say.

My mother uses her hand to show me that notes go up and down. With her hand she sings, *Amazing Grace, How Sweet the Sound*.

I try to copy her, but I can't because my voice cracks, breaks, and hisses like a car radiator. My mother the pro solves it. I will speak all my song lyrics.

Opening night of *The Princess and the Magic Pea*. I peek through the curtain to see if my mother is in the audience. She's not.

Then I see a pair of huge Jackie O sunglasses slip in through the back of the auditorium. Like a missing cast member from a James Bond film, my mother stealthily scopes out her spot, where she can simultaneously watch and escape at the same time. Black hair tied back, trench coat collar up, my mother holds her program to her face, shielding herself—keeping the voices inside and at bay.

I am dressed in a black catsuit, which looks like something Bob Mackie designed. I speak/sing like Rex Harrison about the virtues of my princess daughter. My crown stays on. I'm so loud, you can hear me outside. After the show, I'm mobbed by senior citizens. All the grandmothers say I'm the only actor they could hear. I'm a triumph. Where is my mother? She has escaped. I can't find her.

I know she is proud because she says, *I love you*, when I return.

My mother gives me the only gift she has. How to act like someone else. I get good at it. By the time I graduate high school, my classmates have voted me the most talented in my year. I even sing a song at my graduation. From my seat on the stage, I look for my mother. I am reminded of that risky night years ago in my catsuit and crown, peeking through the curtain. I feel that same hope, that same excitement. I want her to slide in the back of the crowd with her Jackie O sunglasses and trench coat.

My mother doesn't come to hear me sing in front of my largest audience ever; three thousand people. The voices in her head win that year and I lose her piece by piece.

In the years to come, I know my mother's love is real. I feel it in every performance, character I create, and audience applause I receive. The best part of her is with me always.

***

Sean Ewert has a degree in theater from the University of Northern Colorado. He has performed at such venues as Steppenwolf Garage Rep (Chicago, IL), Studio Theatre (Washington, DC), Collaboraction (Chicago, IL), TUTA Theatre (Chicago, IL), Little Theatre of The Rockies (Greeley, CO), Oracle Theatre (Chicago, IL) and Playbill's Virtual Theatre Festival (2020).

He tells his stories in Chicago and Los Angeles at such shows as The Moth (storySLAM Winner "Nostalgia" Los Angeles 2021), USA Today Storytellers Project (Western/Sunbelt and National shows), JAM Creative Stories, This Much Is True, Flick Lit, Bike Winter Chicago, Story Club Chicago (winner audience favorite), Story Salon, The ReBoot, The Laugh Factory, Pour One Out, and The Antidote. When Sean is not on-stage telling stories, he coaches storytellers and leads personal narrative workshops.

Sean works during the day at the Spondylitis Association of America, helping those living with the disease share their stories about being a pain warrior and elevating public awareness of spondyloarthritis. Sean lives with his partner John and rescue dog Pilot.

3 | Retrieving My Belongings by Emily Rich

I had forgotten what a bully the wind could be, how it could blast right into you, through your clothes, hurling sand-like particles of snow up in your face. The red and black car coat I'd bought at a thrift store back in high school was no match for such brutal weather. Nor were the thin canvas high tops, the only closed-toed shoes I owned. Nor, for that matter, were the flimsy walls of the Casper, Wyoming Greyhound bus terminal, where I found myself at three a.m. in the waning days of 1988, temporarily stranded.

It was for lack of a decent winter jacket, among other things, that I was making the 900-mile trek from Denver to my ex-boyfriend's place in Missoula, Montana. He had broken up with me while I was working in the refugee camps of Thailand, but he still had all my stuff, and I was going to get it back.

Of course, that wasn't the only reason I'd bolted out on my highplains adventure. Newly single and on holiday leave from my overseas job, I had nowhere to go but my parent's home, a place I'd intended never to return. Just one day after Christmas, I'd already had enough. The weight of a thousand unpleasant memories lurked in every corner of the old house and piled up in my psyche, leaving me desperate for escape.

I'd dialed Curt from the wall phone in my parents' kitchen. "You've got all my things," I blurted out, following his surprised hello. "My winter clothes, my books, my albums…"

"Okay, come get them," he replied.

"You know I don't have a car. How am I supposed to get to Missoula?"

"See if you can get a flight. I'll get you at the airport."

A last-minute flight from Denver to Missoula was over $800—far more than I had. But I already decided I would retrieve my belongings. I was determined to do so even if it meant boarding a Greyhound bus at midnight, just as the weather was transitioning from snowstorm to blizzard.

There were only a handful of people on the bus when I got on, and I struggled to imagine what compelled these other travelers— small town ranchers and farmers, migrant laborers, miscellaneous drifters—out into the cold on such a night. We travelled in darkened silence, the lights of Denver disappearing into blackness. But less than three hours into the journey, the acrid smell of burning rubber filled the bus's interior, forcing the driver to pull off in the nearest town.

"Engine trouble," our driver informed us. "Nothing to be done at this time of night," he said, herding us into the Casper bus station to wait on a replacement vehicle.

I huddled with the other passengers in the cramped neon-lit waiting area, bunching my inadequate jacket tightly around me. With my hands deep in my pockets, I could feel the letter. I carried it as a promise to my broken heart that I would not forget who had broken up with whom six months earlier.

He was tired of waiting; the letter informed me. He'd finished up the season as a fishing guide in Alaska and had plenty of time to think things over. He was going back to Montana to enroll in law school and get on with his life.

"I've come to accept that you love your job and the future you envision, with a career overseas, which I am not going to share in," the letter continued. "I want you to know I will always remember you as one of the neatest people I have ever met."

"One of the neatest people…" The phrase throbbed in my head like a bruise.

Neatest. Could that be all I meant to him after so much time?

Curt and I were together for five years, from my first week in college through the first year after graduation. We'd moved in together my sophomore year, enduring the wrath of my parents and the ridicule of his Phi Delt brothers who called him "pussy whipped" for decamping from the frat house. When he graduated, one year ahead of me, he stayed in our tiny college town waiting for me to finish my degree.

At the end of my senior year, I got a fellowship to study the impact of rural development in Northern Thailand, and Curt shared my enthusiasm. He would join me after the three-month study period, and we could travel the region before returning to the States to consider what to do with our future.

He had dreams of returning to his home state of Montana—not to Billings, where he'd grown up, but to Missoula.

"It's a great little town," he gushed, excitement filling his sky-colored eyes. "Tons of hiking and mountain biking. You can take graduate classes at the University while I study for the LSATS."

But my Thailand fellowship morphed into a dream-job opportunity: doing casework for war-displaced refugees seeking asylum in the United States. So, rather than travel as planned, Curt took a job in a Bangkok law firm translating documents into "native-speaker-grade" English.

He tried to be a good sport, but he hated living in Bangkok, with all the traffic and the heat, while I spent most of the time up country along the Lao and Cambodian borders. Moreover, at 6'4" and covered with dark body hair, Curt was a walking oddity ("like a fucking gorilla," he said). He attracted stares wherever he went.

He languished. He missed the mountains and fly-fishing rivers of his native state, the change of seasons, the broad horizons, the roads he could travel for miles barely passing another soul. Eight months after he first arrived for our Southeast Asian adventure, he announced he wanted to go home.

We weren't breaking up, we told each other, as Curt folded himself into an early morning taxi to Don Mueang Airport. We were just taking a breather, giving each other some space to think. But in my heart I suspected differently, and as I took the creaking elevator back to our fourth-floor apartment, my chest filled with heaving sadness. I rushed to the balcony to see his taxi as it made its way through the already traffic-clogged streets of Bangkok.

Two empty bottles of Singha beer stood sentry on the balcony table, left over from the night before, where we'd sat in glum silence, staring out into the florescent city night, not talking about what was to come. Now I couldn't bear to remove them. For months they remained in position, labels soaked by the rains, steamed and bleached by the humid sun.

And then the letter came—the oddly distant and formal words on stationary so thin I could run my finger along the backside and feel the imprint of his words telling me goodbye.

Back in the Greyhound station, the little band of disgorged bus passengers sat bleary eyed and mostly silent. Some tried dozing off on the hard plastic seats in the cramped waiting area. Others leaned against their suitcases on the linoleum floor.

Eventually, the driver came in, stamping the snow off his feet at the door. There were no replacement busses available in this weather, he explained. But if we wanted to wait, the south-bound bus would be along in a few hours to take us back to Denver.

For those wanting to continue north, the company had a commuter van that could get us as far as Billings.

I scrunched the letter in my pocket. If I wanted an easy excuse to back out, here was my chance. But when the van pulled up to the station door, I trundled out into the blowing storm with the other die-hard travelers.

For the next several hours, we rattled along the deserted Wyoming highway as the winds barreled against us and the black of the road disappeared beneath the driving snow. We were like a tiny ship buffeted and tossed, making our way through the unlit passage across the high plains. I couldn't imagine feeling more utterly alone.

How many times had Curt and I traveled this road during our years together, cruising along in his tan Honda Civic during summer and winter breaks? It was something we looked forward to despite the distances: eleven hours from our college town to Curt's parents' house in Billings, then another nine to Denver.

We were a little capsule all to ourselves, a cooler of snacks and soda in the back seat, a stack of cassette tapes packed into a wooden crate at my feet. We would talk or sit silently or listen to music. I felt at the time as if that little car contained all I needed in life.

From the time we started dating, I never went back to Denver without Curt. I never explained to him my fear of returning home by myself. He could see that my dad was a foul-tempered asshole. I didn't need to go into detail about the physical abuse I'd endured as a child.

I didn't want to admit, but there was an element of escapism in the work I was doing in Thailand. I'd interviewed hundreds of people whose suffering had been incomparably worse than my own. Cambodians who'd lost entire families during the Khmer Rouge, Laotians who'd spent a generation hiding out in the jungle hills, always on the brink of starvation. Former South Vietnamese military officers released from prison camps so torturous, they trembled uncontrollably trying to recount their stories.

If I was able, I would have gathered up the lot of them and booked them on a plane for the U.S. that afternoon. And why not? What was so wrong with giving people a shot at the thing they thought would make them happy?

But what would make *me* happy? I mused, my head pressed against the dark and chilled window of the Greyhound commuter van. If I had truly found my life's calling, why was I hurtling myself through the frozen-prairie lands of Wyoming and Montana during the dead of winter in the middle of the night? Why had I come back to the States in the first place, knowing I had nowhere comfortable to settle, even for a month-long holiday leave? What was I going to Missoula to retrieve after all? A few paltry belongings?

As the sun rose, the outlines of the city of Billings, Curt's hometown, sharpened into focus in the early morning light. Somewhere out there, beneath the sandstone cliffs that lined the city, Curt's parents' house with its gambrel roof sat nested among the blue spruce trees on its tidy cul-de-sac.

I spent the fondest holidays there with Curt, his parents, brothers and girlfriends, a raucous and happy collection, which gave me a few years of loving memories to paper over the wounds of early life.

There was a nine o'clock bus continuing on to Missoula. I didn't hesitate to board.

I settled into my seat and watched the road roll past, through all the familiar towns along Interstate 90, Columbus, Bozeman, Butte, and finally near nightfall, Missoula.

Curt was there at the station to meet me, standing tall and broad shouldered, his winter parka unzipped over a thick fisherman's wool sweater. He had a cautious smile, but his eyes glowed with happiness and relief. I knew before exchanging a word that he felt what I felt. At last, I was home.

***

Emily Rich is managing editor of the Bay to Ocean Journal, a publication of the Eastern Shore Writers Association. Previously, she served as editor of the Delmarva Review and as nonfiction editor of the Little Patuxent Review. Emily has taught memoir writing at the Writers Center in Bethesda, MD and through the Lighthouse Guild at Salisbury University. Her work has been published in *The Pinch*, *Hippocampus*, and *Cutbank* online, among others. She has twice been listed as a notable in Best American Essays. She lives on the Eastern Shore of Maryland with her husband, Curt. After thirty-three years of marriage, their nest has been emptied of children and refilled with three raucous Labradors.

4 | My First Love by Mary Daurio

Awake or asleep, from the time I was four years old, I dreamed of owning a pony. A lot of little girls shared my dream, but certainly not with the fervor I possessed. One day, at Cookstown Fair, I was sure I would get my years-long wish. A tiny pony stood forlorn in a circus-type cage, and the carnival folk were selling tickets for a chance to win him. I bought a ticket and waited right beside the pony's crate, holding tight to the bars, with my eye on the man drawing the lucky stub from a big whirling drum, but my number never won. That night when saying my prayers, I asked for a pony.

"Mary, prayers are not intended for asking to have a pony," Mom said. She sat on the side of my bed and held my hand in hers. "Thank Him. Ask Him to bless folk and say you're sorry for anything wrong you may have done. We don't ask God for things."

"A pony is not a thing." I got up from my knees, my back straight and stiff.

"That may be true, but we don't ask God for ponies."

I didn't think God cared if I asked him for a pony. There were a lot of ponies in the world. Surely, I could have one.

Until God saw fit to send me a pony, I begged Dad to let me sit on his racehorses as he cooled them down after their workouts, strolling quietly with them on a lead. One day while Dad was walking me around on Brown Velvet, his fastest racer, she startled and jumped sideways as the swallows, protecting their nests, swooped down toward our screeching old tomcat. Dad's arms came from the clear blue sky, swept me off that dancing mare, and placed me onto the soft green grass.

I wasn't afraid, for no harm could come to me in my father's broad arms. The scent of the meadow grounded me on Mother Earth.

But Father's hands were trembling when he set me down amid the fragrant daisies and buttercups.

Shortly after that adventure, my prayers were answered, and my greatest dream came true.

I was so excited. I couldn't sleep the night before, as visions of my pony danced in my head—better than Christmas. We planned on travelling to a nearby farm to get my pony right after breakfast the next day. That morning, the farmer, Mr. Milt, was having two foals delivered from a pony ranch renowned for having the finest ponies in the district. A young friend, Sammy, worked for the summer at the ranch, so he knew the stock and planned on meeting us at the farm to help me pick the better pony. Mr. Milt was keeping one for himself.

Dad opened the car's front door and motioned for Mother and me to hop aboard.

"Aren't you bringing the trailer, Dad?" Was I really getting a pony if he was driving the car there?

"He's only a pony foal, just weaned. I took the back seat out of the car, and he can ride home that way."

I wasn't sure about that, but the back seat reclined on the lawn under the Manitoba maple tree. My parents weren't in the habit of lying to me, so I had no reason to believe my father would now. Still, there was the question of how Santa brought all the gifts at Christmas, which they never answered to my satisfaction. But I let my excitement take over any doubt.

Finally, we arrived at the farm. In a rail-fenced paddock, a plain grey pony stood along with a larger pony that was grey and white, with the colors all swirled together like a marble. We drove close to the paddock, where Sammy waited at the gate. He and I walked among the ponies, leaving the adults at the entrance.

"Mary, if you get a choice, take the bigger fellow. I played with him all summer, and he's the best by far."

The pony turned his head to Sammy, and we both petted him. The little grey was standoffish but allowed me to touch him when Sammy held his halter.

"Mousey here is a good pony, but he nips if given a chance. I hope you get to have the other one." He moved the grey and white over so I could see his haunches. "You could call him Lightning because of that white streak that looks like lightning on his hip," Sammy said as we walked toward the waiting adults.

Lightning followed us right away. Mousey, when left alone, trotted along to join us.

Because Mr. Milt went to the trouble of having the ponies delivered to his place, Dad offered him the first choice. But Mr. Milt made a big production of being a gentleman in this fashion.

"Oh, no, let the little girl go first."

He must have thought I'd take the tiny pony because I was only eight. When I picked the painted pony, his face dropped. Sammy smiled.

We loaded the bigger pony in the back of the car. I wanted to ride in back with him, but Father said that wouldn't be safe, so I watched him with eager eyes for the whole trip from the front seat. That wonderful equine odor filled the car. Mom had her hanky over her nose, but I couldn't breathe deeply enough. Upon arriving home, my pony hopped out of the car and did his business on the gravel drive.

"Well, isn't he a dandy?" Mom said.

Dandy, my first love, arrived at our farm on the fourth concession of Tosorontio township. My initial love for him was an affection, always alive in my heart. Dandy kindled the passion for horses in my soul that I'd inherited from my father. Horses run in the blood. It's a disease, once afflicted, incurable. Blessed benediction.

Mom wasn't in favor of praying to God for a pony, but she was adamant He be thanked for one.

He was. Joyfully.

Thus began our days together, a union of spirits, equine, and human. However, at the start, Dandy was full of feet-flashing energy. When I ran with him in the field one day, he reared toward me. He only wanted to play. That frightened me, and I left him fallow for some time.

Father drew me to him one evening and said, "Mary, you aren't spending time with your pony as you should."

I nodded but didn't own up to my cowardice.

"Darling, each evening when I do chores, brush him. That's all I ask. Or he goes to Doug, who would appreciate him."

Doug, the boy down the road, wasn't getting my pony. I took Father's words to heart and spent every free moment with Dandy. Tied in his stall, he couldn't rear. It was a perfect chance for us to get better acquainted and for me to feel comfortable again.

They say lovers often choose by scent. That is why you see unlikely combinations. Dandy and I were a perfect pair.

That Eau de equine, even today, brings him to mind. I'd sit on him and lay down with his soft mane in my face, smelling the very essence of him. I loved the scent of Dandy, and it clung to me. In class, I'd look at Doug and smell my ponytail in triumph.

Dandy turned and nuzzled me when I brushed his silky coat, but he never bit me, and by spring, we'd bonded. With him wearing my Christmas bridle, we rode over the fields.

Life had been lonely on the farm with my siblings married and gone. I was the only child left at home. My four older sisters had children of their own, and my parents were grandparents. Now I had a friend, someone to share my secrets and dreams. He would flick his ears listening attentively to my every notion.

My patient pony stood, his head turned, gazing back at me, never moving a muscle while I vaulted over his rump and onto his back—a great stunt. Then we'd be off to spend hot summer days swimming or communing under the willow trees at the river. Sometimes we would hunker down in the long grass and snooze.

We had another trick, usually done when Mother was away. Dandy would walk up the front porch steps into the house and eat an apple off the kitchen table. Father once told her, "We had company while you were in town."

She rolled her eyes and laughed when he revealed the truth.

My nieces and nephews were hoisted onto Dandy's broad back, three at a time, for rides when they visited. Dandy never minded. But I did. I felt a twinge of jealousy, sharing my only love.

He took to my harness training but eventually grew out of the little cart we had for him. That was just as well, for I was growing too. Now in high school, I met a girl who lived two roads over. She rode a big appaloosa to our farm one day, and Dandy and I went out with her.

With her long dangling whip, she started hitting Dandy over and over on his shoulder and front legs. Not fiercely, but hard enough.

"Stop it," I said. My Dandy had never seen a whip.

"Sure." She started hitting my legs instead.

In one fierce, ferocious lunge, with ears back and teeth barred, Dandy almost chomped her thigh, but he listened when I drew him back with the reins. Her horse jumped sideways, and she hollered, "You should warn a person that your pony is vicious."

"You're the vicious one. My pony is a better friend to me than I've been to him. He wouldn't stand by and let you abuse me."

Dandy got an extra apple that night, and when he nuzzled me all over, I knew he forgave my lapse in defending him. We never rode with that girl again.

All I learned about love, I learned from Dandy. The joy, the obligation, and the pain of love rest in your heart like a songbird singing sweet plaintiff tunes of joy and anguish.

The year I turned fifteen, Dandy became ill, and the glorious crest on his neck flopped over, heralding what was to come. He wouldn't eat and lost weight. Unable to figure out his malady, we took him to Guelph Veterinary College, where I begged to stay with my sick pony. A kind veterinarian there said I couldn't do that. He could see my love for Dandy in my eyes and said he would take good care of him for me. I know he did.

Once we arrived home, each time the phone rang, I prayed it would be the veterinarian from Guelph with good news. The call eventually came, and by the tone of Father's voice and his stricken look, I knew the sad news before he finished talking with the veterinarian. Father told me the doctor was very sorry they'd lost him. There was no cure, and we never knew what Dandy succumbed to or why.

I drowned in tears that long winter following Dandy's death. Finally, spring arrived. I walked along the river where we used to swim and stood under the shade tree he so enjoyed, saying my goodbyes. Knowing why he died wouldn't have helped relieve my grief. When I reached the other side of that sorrow, the love we'd shared left me with intense gratitude for Dandy and everything I'd learned from him.

He taught me to have patience for myself and others, perseverance, and reverence for life, and appreciation for the treasure and burden of friendship. We may not be able to keep our loved ones forever, but they stay etched on our hearts and souls. The love we hold for them is never gone. It does not rush off into the ether when their spirits leave this realm. It stays to build the foundation for dealing with all other loves and losses. We all live on in love. Love can never be lost.

***

Mary Daurio is a grandmother studying creative writing at Brock University while working on a short-story compilation about her experiences driving racehorses.

She is editing her novels, one an untitled racetrack mystery and a coming-of-age story, *Time and Chance*. She writes for joy and is pleased when people enjoy her stories. Mary's work has appeared online and in print in *Friday Flash Fiction*, *Cafelit*, *Medium*, *Pure Slush anthologies*, *The Fictional Café*, *Harrowsmith Magazine*, *Spillwords*, *Adelaide*, and *Sweet Cat Press*.

5 | The Verb to Mother by Mary Dean Cason

My children are adopted. Not because I'm the benevolent sort who goes around picking up street urchins, but because I totally sucked at getting pregnant. It started with an ectopic pregnancy in 1980 that almost ended me. It caused so much damage I wound up getting fertility treatments for years, some of which involved my husband shooting me up with hormones. He was a dentist. Great with needles in the mouth, not so much in the ass. Trying to get pregnant might be fun for lots of couples—but taking your temperature, having sex according to a calendar, going through in vitro, rushing to the clinic with sperm in a jar—not so much. There was a point back in 1982 when I was hopped up on enough follicle-stimulating hormones to make a stud horse in Kentucky hard.

There's a line I read once: *You have to be the verb before you can be the noun.* As well as being the oldest of five, being a pediatric occupational therapist, surely, I'd mastered the verb to mother well in advance of becoming one.

Eventually I got lucky—not pregnant—but lucky. We adopted Matthew in Chippewa Falls, Wisconsin in 1983. He was perfect. We were ecstatic. Friends threw us a baby shower, the grandparents flew in, and we sprang out of bed for two o'clock feedings.

There were the odd smacks across the face, of course. *What do you know about his real mother? Did you get a medical history, social? Fetal alcohol syndrome is rampant in Wisconsin, you know.* But most of the time people said how much he looked like me, or his dad.

"Actually, he's adopted," I often found myself saying.

"Wow, he's huge and you're so tiny?"

I'd laugh and say, "Matt's adopted."

"What beautiful green eyes," and I'd volunteer that he didn't get them from me. He was adopted. Why was I compelled to tell total strangers about my son's origins?

On the way back from the zoo, when he was two-and-a-half, we stopped at a playground. I parked the stroller by a bench where a woman was breastfeeding a little boy not much younger than Matt. She was a full-figured, full exposure breast feeder. They were common in the eighties, silently shouting, *it is my right, goddamn it, to whip out the only natural and scientifically proven delivery system of nutrition for the human child—wherever and whenever I please. AND just try to stop me!* I wouldn't have dared.

The little boy hopped off his mother's knee and into the sandbox with Matt. My son, however, was far more taken with the woman's breast than the buckets and shovels, that he approached her, reaching out a finger to touch her. She scowled at my little boy as she covered herself saying, "You'd think he'd never seen a breast before."

Well, not one the size of a hot air balloon, I thought, but of course did not say.

"He looks just past weaning himself," she said.

Matt hadn't used a bottle in a year.

"Is he weaned?" the woman looked at my small chest with a hint of pity. I thought about it for a moment. After all, this was my cue. But my answer shocked even me.

"Actually, I didn't breastfeed him."

Shock and downright incredulity overtook the woman's face. "Oh, my God," she said. "You must be worried sick. The immunities!"

And the truth was it bothered me. It hurt like hell that I hadn't been able to carry this beautiful little boy inside me, experience his birth, and have him feed at my breast while passing along my supermom immunities. But this woman was a bitch.

Her son hopped back up on her lap and asked for more "nummy." Once again, she whipped it out and the lip-smacking magnet latched on.

God, Lady, I wanted to say. *If a kid can hop up, take the thing in both hands and tilt his head back like he's draining a long neck, he's ready for a sippy cup.*

Then I did it. "Actually," I looked at the woman. "He's adopted." I said it this one last time because I wanted to make her feel bad. I expected some retraction that would involve how wonderful baby formula was these days.

"I have a niece who's adopted," she said as her little boy went back to the sandbox.

"Nice, how old?" I gathered my son's things, signaling it was time to head home.

"Fourteen."

I softened. "They live around here?" I smiled as I clicked Matt into the stroller.

"Well, the parents are in Evanston." She buttoned her blouse. "But the kid's in rehab." She stood and yanked her son out of the sandbox. "You know how it is. You never really know what you're gonna get."

I'd promised myself I'd watch my language around Matt. They're parrots at two-and-a-half. I must have fallen off the wagon because later that day, I heard the giraffe call the elephant a "fucking bitch."

A month later, my daughter arrived. Precious Emma was born on a Friday and home on Monday. She was tiny, with big, black button eyes. Her birth mother is Irish. Her birth father is half Puerto Rican, half Pakistani. I'd never seen a more beautiful child.

She was just weeks old when I ran out to the store one stormy October night. I cradled her in the top of the cart all swaddled in fleecy pink. As I was making my way through the checkout, a cart hit me from behind. Just a slight tap on the rear, so I turned. The man behind me apologized. "So sorry," he said. Then he saw my baby. "Jeez, she's beautiful. How old?"

"Two weeks," I said, beaming. I expected the questions "Boy, she must look like her dad. You're so fair and look at that dark hair and olive skin." But that's not what I got.

"Two weeks! God, you look great." He gave me a head to toe. "Sorry, but you do. Two weeks? Jeez." He was a nice-looking guy, slender, wearing a suit and tie. I just smiled and began lifting the Pampers, baby wipes, and formula onto the belt. Lightening flashed outside while torrents of rain fell.

"Two weeks?" he said it again. "I gotta kid, a little boy, just past two, and my wife is really struggling to lose the weight. She swears breastfeeding does the trick, but I see you're using formula."

What an intrusive ass. I gave the man a wan smile and got out my wallet.

"Two weeks." I couldn't believe he said it again. "You do yoga?"

I turned to the man, lifting the hood of my raincoat over my head. "Yeah, yoga," I said. "Works miracles—in just two weeks."

What a jerk.

I left the store, draping my coat over Emma who snoozed away. As I dodged puddles, I thought maybe I should go back and tell the guy. I mean, maybe he was a real ass. Maybe he was going to go home and yell at his wife: *Hey, I just saw this woman in the grocery store. Had a two-week-old kid. Looked damn good. I think it's time you hit the gym, babe!*

No! Not my problem. Simply not my concern. I do not have to tell every Tom, Dick, and Harry I meet at the park, or in the grocery store that my kids are adopted.

I got to the car, clicked Emma into her car seat and unloaded the groceries. Just as I was about to start the car, it needled me again. What if he's a terrible guy? I mean, you hear crazy things. On the news and in the papers, you see stuff that makes you cringe. A perfectly normal guy goes home, slams the door. *Hey, bitch! I've had it with the fat ass and the roll around the middle. A chick at the store, has a two-week-old, looks like a million bucks. Lay off the Oreos—or I'm outa here!*

The hatch of the car next to me slammed. Through the rain, I could see it was the guy. *Okay*, I said to myself. *This is the last time. I swear to God I will never tell another stranger my kids are adopted. But this guy's wife deserves a break.* I had friends who had C-sections and really struggled to get their bodies back.

It was dark and pouring, but I hurried around to the driver's side of the car next to me. The hood of my jacket gave me tunnel vision with wisps of hair plastered to my face. I knocked on the window. It took another rap on the glass before the window went down. "Hey, bud," I said. "About what went on in there, there's something you don't understand." All of a sudden, the interior car lights went on and I could see the guy was sitting on the passenger side. I was talking to his wife.

"Oh, really?" The woman's head was bobbing. "Exactly what went on in there between you two that you gotta tell my husband?" She looked at him, then back at me. "What is it?"

And then it clicked. She didn't recognize me, but the woman from the park was one of those women you don't forget. I looked over at the guy, and he was dying. He gave me this look that said, *please, lady, don't, please.* It occurred to me that maybe they deserved each other. Again, the woman asked me what I want to tell her husband. And I had nothing. I was as blank as a sheet of paper. I looked over the hood of the car and I saw a sign on the grocery store window.

"Milk," I said, looking across the woman at her husband. "Didn't you say something about your kid needing milk?" I pointed to the store. "Two-ninety-nine a gallon." I tapped goodbye on the roof of the car and sprinted. I ran like hell to my car. Yoga or no yoga, I was no match for a big, angry woman who might want to kill the messenger first and her husband later.

But I didn't get in the front seat. I slid into the back seat. I unbuckled my baby and pulled her into my arms. And I sobbed into her soft pink hat. I cried because I finally realized all that sadness and pain I'd been holding because I hadn't been able to carry my own babies, had not been able to give them immunities, and because I'd never known the pain and miracles of their births—was about me. They were fine. They were perfect and loved and happy.

The car next to me drove away. I kissed my daughter's head and knew in my bones that if either of my children ever got some horrid illness—that my immunities might have protected them from—I would move heaven and earth, and even hell to make them well. Protection is the prime mover of the verb, to mother.

My children survived the fevers and bruises of childhood. Six-foot four Matt is my hero, funny, successful, and uncommonly generous. Emma is still petite, tough, kind, smart, and so strikingly beautiful that strangers turn in the street. Had I been a wizard, I could never have conjured up more complex, fascinating, loving children.

***

Mary Dean Cason grew up in North Carolina, where she over-indulged on Eudora Welty, Zora Neal Hurston, Lee Smith, and later Ellen Gilchrist. She made her way to Chicago where a series of careers—flight attendant, occupational therapist, medical writer, and best of all, mother—gave her "material aplenty." Her short story, *What Solomon Saw*, became a finalist in Chicago Public Radio's Stories on Stage and spurred her to enroll at the University of Chicago's Writers Studio where she won the 2008 prize for fiction. *What Solomon Saw and Other Stories* is available on Amazon.com.

Mary Dean has been a featured writer/performer at several Chicago's live-lit venues including This Much is True and Story Sessions, as well as co-founding the San Miguel de Allende International Storytelling Festival. She's thrilled that *Banished Daughters of Eve*, a novel she's currently pitching to agents, recently took second place in the Chicago Writers Association First Chapter Contest. In her day job, Mary Dean is a medical writer specializing in communications with surgeons.

6 | The Sound of Silence by Ellen Blum Barish

My husband and I were having dinner out, lucky to have snagged a sitter for our two middle-school age children, when I saw an older couple at a nearby table sitting quietly, not speaking. I elbowed him, and with a critical tone in my voice, whispered, "See those two over there? I hope we'll never be like that. We'll always have something to talk about, right?"

David nodded, letting me stew in my judgment. He didn't argue, as he had heard that sermon before. If there wasn't a steady flow of conversation with one's partner, I'd preach, one's marriage was headed for trouble.

It was my conviction for good reasons. Just a year after our wedding, my parents ended their twenty-seven-year marriage, due in part to a lack of communication. Second, language matters to me. A lot. My husband and I earned degrees in Communication Studies and landed in professions where finding the right words is essential. We deconstructed movies, menus, and music. We dug into the psyches of family and friends. We sometimes read aloud to one another in bed. Talking was *our thing*.

I may put too much stock in words because I rely on them as a writer, but I believe in the power of dialogue for keeping a marriage strong. Words are the synovial fluid between us, keeping us connected and flexible, even if only by a thread during the most stressful times.

And there were many of those.

In the early 1980s, when David was focusing on finishing law school and passing the Bar exam and I was earning my master's in journalism, there was little time for date nights, let alone conversation. I was worried that we'd lose our connection. So, I offered the idea of Sunday morning meetings in which we'd map out who was where that week over our morning coffee.

"You're at the library Tuesday and I'll be on campus that night, so maybe I can pick you up and we can get dinner on the way home?" Though these exchanges weren't as riveting as in the past, I was relieved that David was game, and those check-ins kept us on task and in sync.

However, the flow of conversation became even trickier in the 1990s when we moved from intellectual to physical challenges. The years I was pregnant and we were both adjusting to new parenthood top that list. Managing our professional lives and our small new family business left us with little energy for anything beyond what was front and center. Our dialogues were more like barter: "If you can pick Jenny up at soccer practice, I can take your suits to the cleaners. If you drop Emily off at work, I can prep dinner." During these years we were giving everything we had to our children, our verbal interactions were all business. This concerned me enough to drag us over to a therapist where we got back to talking, but not in the free-flowing way we had before. It was hard work–more like a psycho-archeological dig–but it kept the pages of our life together turning.

In the 2000s, when our eldest daughter spent some time in the hospital and David had a diagnosis of diabetes along with a heart condition, a conversation gap formed between us. I wanted to talk through it, but David didn't have words then. What little talk we exchanged took on a new tone. A bit more accusing. A little more defended. Both of us were just a little more sensitive. "With your heart and blood sugar at risk, do you really want to eat that?" I'd admonish.

He'd stare back. "Did I ask your opinion?"

Where was our easy banter and art-fueled tete-a-tetes? We had been hit hard by health issues and it had taken a toll. I fretted that like my parents, we might not make it.

But thankfully, we hung in there and in the 2010s, health issues improved. Our daughters had moved out of the house. We were feeling professionally re-energized and recognized a desire to return to previous passions. David got back on his bike and onto the disc golf course, and I dove deeper into writing and publishing. But because we were busy, our conversations were relegated to texts, emails, errands in the car and the occasional dinner out.

Him: "Want to bike to the blues festival in Grant Park next month?"

Me: "How does next Sunday look for hosting a barbeque?"

I was pleased about the plans but missed the sound of our voices, the easy-breezy chitchat of our youth. I was anxious, as this conjured my long-held fear of married silence.

Around that time, we stumbled upon a gathering of lively local storytellers and fell in love with them and telling stories on stage. These writers and performers were sharing stories from their lives–often very personal ones–and the monthly meetups provided gentle but productive feedback. David and I were moved to share pieces about our childhood and raising children, losing family members, and some stories about our marriage. In addition to the thoughtful input, we got a unique chance to return to the big moments in our life in a new way. We were revisiting them, retelling them, and reframing them. We were spilling over with self-discovery and having fun in the process! It was, after all, about words.

It's healthy for two people in a long marriage to go in and out of sync, as natural as the beat of a heart or the inhale or exhale of a breath. Language had, for the most part, done the hard work of keeping us connected during the tough times.

Or had it?

On an unusually temperate Saturday evening with no plans, we found ourselves by the firepit in our backyard. We were tired but contented. I was already in my pajamas, wrapped in a blanket, sipping a glass of white wine. David was in shorts and his straw fedora, drinking an IPA. Having just finished supper, we had sunk into our patio chairs, and set three logs burning. I was studying the light in the flame, listening to the crackle of the kindling, enjoying the warmth of the wine and the blanket. David was staring into the fire, not on his phone or watching TV. We were lost in watching the flames dance, fully present, together, but silent. It felt really good. Warm. Cozy. Safe. And comfortable.

If someone had been watching us, that person would have thought, *now there's a couple with nothing to talk about.* Exactly like those older married folks I critiqued in restaurants.

Although the scene may not have shown it, we were connecting. Without saying a word. I thought, *who else in the world could I do this with? Who else would I want to do this with?*

That's the moment when the spark hit: Communication isn't only about language. Its root comes from the Latin *communicare* which means to *share, exchange, or be in relation with.* One can successfully communicate with a loved one *without* words. Silence between long-married people isn't necessarily a sign of having nothing to say to one another. It may be a sign of having already said it and choosing to stay. Not talking is not necessarily a sign of indifference. It may be a sign of intimacy.

Love can live contentedly in the sound of silence.

Several hours later, we slowly rose, checked the embers, covered the pit, and headed wordlessly up to bed.

***

Ellen Blum Barish is the author of *Seven Springs* (Shanti Arts, 2021), *Views from the Home Office Window* (Adams Street Publishing, 2007) and a contributor to a previous anthology, published by Chicago Story Press, Inc. You can find her essays in the *New York Times*, *The Chicago Tribune*, *Tablet*, *Lilith*, *Brevity*, *Full Grown People*, *Literary Mama* and hear them on Chicago Public Radio. She founded the literary publication *Thread*, which earned four notables in *Best American Essays*, and has taught writing at Northwestern University where she earned a master's in journalism. She teaches writing workshops around the country and works privately with writers on essay collections and memoirs.

7 | Parts of Her by Christine Wopat

Last week, I looked in the mirror and saw my father looking back at me.

I studied my reflection. It was the crow's feet around my eyes that did it, the way they crinkled when I smiled. I saw my father's nose, a big one that prompted everyone to call me "Nosey-girl" in 8th grade for an entire month. I saw his eyes, too far set out in my face, his mouth full of crowded teeth, his thinning hair.

Rounding the bend to forty, I am the spitting image of him. Staring back at me is not only my father, but my biggest fear: screwing up this gift of parenthood that I fought so hard for. After years of infertility, my twins died at birth and my living daughter and son are just beginning to ask questions. In that reflection, I saw and felt disgust. *If I become like him, I could lose my children just like he lost me.*

I was twenty-one when my parents divorced. I went home for a weekend to have my wisdom teeth removed, afterward recovering in my parents' bed watching old VHS tapes. My parents were arguing, as they almost always were. It didn't matter what it was about; they didn't agree. My father used cruelty to get his point across, and he would not back down until my mom acquiesced.

Sometimes that meant my mom heading to her room alone to sort through her coin collection, other times it meant throwing something (her keys, a glass, a plate), once it meant a crookedly thrown steak knife lodged into the coffee table, but it always resulted in me burrowed in my closet with the door shut, my Walkman turned up to the highest volume, pretending everything was fine.

This fight felt different, though, because it was my father who left at the end. The argument was about going to dinner with the neighbors. My mom didn't want to leave me. My dad said I was, "just being a fucking baby," and I'd be fine at home alone. He left and went to dinner with the neighbors by himself. This behavior was new.

I went back to college that Monday, and I never set foot in my childhood home again. I was happiest at college anyway, pretending nothing was wrong. By the time I was ready to face the situation and him, the locks were changed. The house had new owners, my things discarded into a storage shed, perhaps a dumpster, or given to charity. He had moved in with the lady from across the street. Apparently, that dinner was the start of something big.

For a while, I tried to have a relationship with him, despite warnings from my mother and sister. He showed up to help me change a burnt-out taillight in an icy Walmart parking lot, sent me a Christmas gift in the mail, and paid my phone bill. I was hopeful this could be the beginning of a better relationship.

But as I grew weary of being stuck in the middle of my parent's divorce chaos, I pulled back from him. Then the threats began, and everything unraveled. He screamed at me on the phone, then stopped paying the bill. He accused me of forging his signature on a federal document, sued my sister for student loans, and in a hastily scrawled email, let us know unequivocally that we owed him all the money he used to raise us. As a post-script, he mentioned my sister wasn't his "real daughter," a fact everyone knew except for my sister and me. He showed up at my college graduation without a ticket and was forced to wait in the lobby. He stood there glaring at me. I did not tell him about my upcoming wedding.

Later, I tried again. Married, I felt more grown-up, and convinced myself I could handle it. We sat through awkward dinners together, with my husband trying heroically to spark up a conversation between us.

"He really seems okay," Brian said once. "I just don't get it. Just a normal guy."

I stared at him. "You do *not* know him, trust me."

But then, I wondered: is he right? I might be overreacting. Perhaps I'm wrong to keep him away. I may have imagined the threats, insults, gaslighting, and the untethered anger. After all, you are supposed to love your parents no matter what. And if I loved him, why couldn't I just give him another chance?

I called my best friend from high school. "What do you remember about my dad?"

"Well, he was terrifying. I remember that much," she said. "You're not making it up, if that is what you're asking. Remember when he almost got into a fistfight with one of our classmates? Oh, and the time when we both had to hide in your closet from him after you accidentally let the dog out?"

I remembered.

The last time I sent him an email was in May 2015 when I ran a half-marathon, and in a fit of weakness emailed him about it. I was still looking for acknowledgment all those years later. Disappointed in my moment of fragility, I tried not to think about getting a response. I didn't need it. He never called or wrote again.

But then, thoughts of our estrangement escalated around holidays or major life events. Was he alone? Did he have someone there to open gifts with him or share a holiday ham? Had I invented the belief that he was cruel as a mechanism to relieve the guilt of our estrangement, or was he straight-up mean? Did I get it all wrong? Shouldn't I love him, anyway?

There have always been more questions than answers.

My mom told me he moved to a new state, or at least that's what she heard. Suddenly, I was crippled again by fear and guilt. Was it worth it, the estrangement? What had I gained? Had I really protected myself? Was I missing out on a loving relationship? What was this all for?

In the end, I reminded myself, *he* was the one who stopped writing.

And then, after the latest round of days steeped with grief and doubt and sadness, wondering why I couldn't just find it in my heart to love my father, something happened. I was in my writing office, moving books from one shelf to another when something fell to the ground. Reaching down to pick it up, I was surprised to see a photo. I had no idea where it came from or how it got lodged inside a book. The photo was of my paternal grandmother, my favorite person of all time. I hadn't seen a photograph of her in years, and my hands trembled. She had been my person. Her tiny, old house next to mine served as my safe haven, her big strong arms and her soft-spoken tones provided my safety net.

After my prematurely born twins died, I attended grief therapy. The therapist suggested that when I spiraled into traumatic memories, I should imagine a place where I felt happy.

"It can be anywhere, anytime, even if you've only been there once."

I pictured my grandmother's dining room. It was New Year's Eve, dark and freezing cold, and my parents were at a party somewhere. The television was in the dining room, where my grandparents spent most of their day. Although I wanted to watch the *Sound of Music*, I was sleepy. My grandmother put three of her dining room chairs in a row, so I could fall asleep when I wanted. When I awakened in the morning, she was asleep in her stiff, hard, dining room chair right next to me. Love enveloped me in one single moment.

When things were bad, or whenever I was especially frightened of my father, it was her house I visited. We read books together and listened to Patsy Cline croon on the record player. We cooked and did crossword puzzles, and she would communicate that I was safe there. She never said those actual words, but she let me know that in every possible way.

I'd often sleep there, huddled up on her scratchy Davenport, the splintered sounds of the Chicago Cubs game coming from my grandfather's old clock radio. Sometimes at night when I couldn't sleep, I dared myself to go up to the attic alone, overwhelmed by the dank-smelling combination of mothballs and mildew. I opened chests of drawers and boxes of holiday decorations, feeling comforted by all the things that my grandmother collected over the years. Her things surrounded me with her love.

My grandmother and I often sat in silence on the rickety wooden swing in her yard, gliding slowly back and forth. The silence was like chocolate cake, delicious to both of us. The anger and the noise surrounded us in both households, although my grandfather lost his steam in his old age. I don't recall my grandma talking to me about the anger, but she was aware. She never asked what was wrong when I ran to her house, sobbing. She just knew, and she loved me through it.

I studied the picture. Her big, beautiful schnoz, gorgeous, too-big eyes, uneven teeth, and thinning hair. She was generous, loving, and kind, someone who provided me with a safe place. Her portrait reminded me of how I sat with her for hours on the porch swing, not talking but simply existing together. In this picture, I saw love.

I'm just like *her*, I thought with relief. I am becoming her. Parts of her are helping me raise my children. If nothing else, my dad had given me her love. And it was her love that I should remember.

***

Christy Wopat is a teacher and writer who never wants anyone to feel alone. Her award-winning memoir, *Almost a Mother: Love, Loss, and Finding Your People When Your Baby Dies*, was published by Orange Hat Publishing in 2018, followed by *Always Ours*, an illustrated picture book about remembering our loved ones, and *After All: Pregnancy After Your Baby Dies*, which was published in 2022.

Her personal essays have been featured in *Still Standing Magazine* and The Educator's Room, among others. Christy also chairs the Events Committee for the Wisconsin Writers Association and is an active member of the Society of Children's Books Writers and Illustrators.

A 4th-grade public school teacher, she lives with her husband and kids in Holmen, Wisconsin.

8 | My Valentine by Michael Quinn

Billy was a puppeteer. I remember the first time I saw him performing in a small theater downtown. He came out dressed in black, and barefoot, carrying a little naked marionette—it was startling how expressive that crude puppet's movements were. Or rather, Billy made it move like that. Even though he was standing right there, the puppet made you forget all about him. Afterward, all I could think about were Billy's downcast eyes and the way his huge lower lip stuck out in concentration. It was a face I wanted to see up close.

Learning he was single, and where he hung out—he mentioned these things in an interview I read—I thought about trying to "accidentally" run into him. But since it was almost February, I instead decided to send him a valentine at his studio address. I incorporated a photo of myself into the card's design—a giant paper locket with a long paper chain—and covered it with a piece of wax paper so it was nearly invisible. I invited Billy to dinner and included my phone number. *P.S.*, I wrote, *Fortune favors the brave!* As soon as I dropped the valentine in the mail, strangely I forgot about it.

A few weeks later, I heard the buzz of an incoming text in the middle of the night. My cat Buffy was sleeping next to me, and our eyes opened at the same time. The surprise in hers must have mirrored my own.

Billy had been traveling and had just gotten back in town. When could we meet? I picked a time-forgotten bistro in Manhattan. Ready hours early, I walked from my apartment in Brooklyn, despite the heavy rain. As I crossed the bridge, umbrella in hand, the city rising up on either side of me, I felt like an inexperienced tightrope walker about to plunge to his death.

There was no one in the restaurant. I couldn't decide whether to sit at a table or wait at the bar, and as I agonized, Billy crossed the street, talking on his phone. He looked annoyed as he hung up, but his expression changed when he saw me through the glass doors. My heart raced. He pushed past the hostess and kissed me on the lips.

"Who are you?" he asked.

Halfway through dinner, Billy got up to change seats. "I want to admire your beauty from this side," he said.

Even though this was a date I'd initiated, I ignored his advances, acting as if I was there on a professional assignment, like a reporter or a detective. He seemed out of reach to me—I'd placed him on a pedestal. But right from the start, Billy treated me like his equal. He didn't seem to regard the circumstances of our meeting as strange at all. He mentioned a new puppet he was building, then took his napkin, transforming it into a white cat that jumped onto my lap and crept toward my crotch.

"I have a cat," I said.

Billy did, too, a mouser named Boots he kept in his studio.

"So," Billy said, "wanna meet Boots?" He offered his arm as we left the restaurant, something no man had ever done before, and as we walked, I felt on the verge of a life changing experience.

After that first night, we saw each other whenever Billy was in town. He would clutch his chest or pretend to fall to the ground whenever he saw me coming. We'd have long dinners while we talked about art, astrology, and theosophy. My interest in these things reminded Billy of his first boyfriend, and the tenderness he felt toward that lost youth illuminated me like the glow of candlelight. He treated me like I was something precious and rare, opening doors for me and holding my hand whenever we walked down the street. Once I found him sitting on my stoop where he handed me a long-stemmed rose he'd fashioned from a smoothed-out wad of aluminum foil. I hadn't been expecting him; he'd been waiting for me a long time. Later in bed, he told me he'd knocked on all my neighbors' doors looking for me like a possessed man.

"You have no idea how powerful you are," he said, as if I'd conjured him there against his will.

But I didn't feel powerful. The only powerful thing was my feelings for him.

One morning, as Billy walked me from his studio to the train, I noticed the city coming to life the way it always does after a long winter. I explained I'd never liked spring; that it depressed me for some reason.

"Let me change your mind about it," Billy said. "Spend spring with me."

Tulips were in bloom when I met him in Philadelphia. He was late picking me up at the train station, where I saw a poster advertising his new show and studied the new puppets' faces, searching for traces of their creator. Then I saw Billy running through the crowd, looking for me. He drank in the sight of me like a man dying of thirst. We ran for the car, slamming the doors shut against the rain. The windows filled with steam as we embraced. We kissed like we were trying to push all of ourselves into the other. I took his face in my hands and held it, trying to slow the onslaught of intensity.

Billy left the hotel early to get to the theater that night. The show was about a love triangle. At the end, the doomed lover died with a broken heart, not because of it, and his ghost rose high above the proscenium, as pieces of tissue paper snow fell slowly to the ground. I went backstage afterward, bursting with pride. When Billy introduced me as "my friend," I was so deflated. I couldn't remember anyone's name.

That night over dinner, Billy told me about the first puppet he'd ever made. It was the one I'd first seen him perform with. He brought it with him everywhere. Once, in a rush, he'd lost the puppet's leg in a snowbank. He spent the night searching for it and found it just before sunrise.

"Couldn't you have just made a new one?" I asked.

Billy looked at me, opened his mouth as if to answer, then stopped. He knocked back his drink and held up his finger for the check. By the time we got back to the room, he had changed. He was combative in bed. Even as he drew me to him, he was pushing me away. There was something impersonal and ugly in the way he looked at me. I could have been anybody. I felt used, diminished, rubbed out, raw.

***

The next morning, Billy was in a rush to get back to the city. He drove and asked me to navigate, then snatched away his phone. He abruptly pulled over, hung over the steering wheel, and cried.

"My work!" Billy shouted, as if I was asking him to choose.

That's it, I thought. *It's over*. All I could think about was getting out of the car. Walking and feeling the sun has always made me feel better. When we got back to the city, Billy grabbed my arm as I opened the door.

"Stay with me," he begged.

In his basement studio, he threw himself on top of me, sobbing. His bulk numbed my body. I watched the sun come sideways through a little window and patted his back as the room grew dark.

Through our ups and downs, Billy wanted to leave but couldn't, and I wanted him to stay but wouldn't make him. One night, blissful and content, he nuzzled into me as we drifted off to sleep.

"I love you," he said.

I'd never told him I loved him because I didn't want to scare him away. Now that he'd brought this feeling out into the open, I knew it was only a matter of time before he tested its limits.

One night, he seemed jittery and distracted when I arrived at his apartment. It was my first and only time there. He said he hadn't slept the night before. The reason was he'd been with someone else. Billy took out his puppet to act out his feelings of remorse because he thought he could express himself better that way. It was a once-in-a-lifetime private show. But when the puppet rubbed its little hand along my face to comfort me, I knew I'd never see Billy again. Not because he cheated, but because he needed to be free.

I remember one night smoothing Billy's brow as he drifted off to sleep.

"Do you know how special you are?" I asked.

He smiled with his eyes closed. "I do," he said. "But you're special, too. You must have known it since you were a child."

I put my head on his chest, sorry for the little boy I'd been who hadn't built a life with that understanding.

That next morning, I left Billy a French poem to translate. He was fluent. It was the prologue in a book I was reading about love, existentialism, and sadness. I left it tucked under a plate on the kitchen table. I knew he would be gone by the time I got back.

Billy surprised me by neatly making my bed. The note he left was crumpled and smeared with oily fingerprints, littered with crumbs from the cookies I'd left him: "I'm crazy about you. Hang tight. Soon."

On the bottom of the page, he had drawn a tiny black heart.

***

Michael Quinn, a memoir writer and book critic, is a frequent contributor to *The Gay & Lesbian Review*, where he once wrote about his experience with Italian fashion and same-sex love in 1990s New York. His memoir piece, *Boo*, about struggling to find the right way to mourn a dead ex-boyfriend, was a finalist for the 2021 Brooklyn Film & Arts Nonfiction Prize. Michael has created performance pieces out of his writing with his longtime collaborator Jeff Allyn Szwast, reading the stories aloud and illustrating them, not with pictures, but with songs. In 2016, they performed an early version of *My Valentine* at New York's legendary experimental theater, Dixon Place. Poet Jenny Williamson wrote, "If you ever get a chance to see this duo perform, seize it with both hands. They will simultaneously break your heart and make you feel redeemed." Michael also writes about books for *Publishers Weekly*, in a monthly column for the Brooklyn newspaper *The Red Hook Star-Revue*, and on his website: mastermichaelquinn.com.

9 | Making Room by Brie Deyton

My fingers plunged into a bowl full of congealed milk under a pile of clothes on the dresser as I looked for my math homework. As I extracted my hand from my sister's cereal bowl, which I estimated was about two weeks old, I began to plan. Despite being one of the few times I had the bedroom my sister and I shared to myself, all I wanted was to get out. I craved space. There just weren't places to go.

Our trailer had two bedrooms, the second being my mother's. The living room and kitchen were connected, and someone was always in one. I'd rarely had the bathroom to myself since we'd moved in, except that time after my sister read my diary when I tore out all the pages into tiny pieces and flushed them down the toilet. It never occurred to me to go outside unless it was to sit out front with my mother in the quiet hours before high school and her workday while she drank coffee in her robe. My mother had made it clear we were not to wander the park. She worked most evenings, and I was wary of people. So I stayed inside.

I turned my sights on the shed—the small addition off the hallway, attached to what had once been a second entrance to the trailer. It was a thin-walled structure with all-weather carpet that housed the belongings my mother had managed to keep hold of from move to move, but for which there was no room. A storehouse of our former lives. Our world became tighter and tighter while my mother kept trying to push out on the walls. Though we collectively saved change in a piggy bank we'd clear out for boardwalk pizza and skee ball at the shore for an afternoon, my mother insisted we would make college happen. At the mall, she'd take us to the jewelry store window and ask which piece we would choose if we had the money to buy it. After we each pointed to one, she'd imagine what it would look like when we wore it to some fancy event when we were older. There was always a new reality to be found.

Mail-order catalogs were special to my mother; a place to find something out of the ordinary for birthdays or for Christmas. She would save for months to purchase something just right. Any lone purchase resulted in a steady stream of more catalogs arriving in the mail. I started racing to the mailbox at the center of the park every day on the way home from school to get the mail. I poured over the pages, picking out all the items I'd need to make my new room perfect. I sketched out floor plans, showed my mother my renderings, and tried to convince her how great it could be. I created a budget and calculated the time it would take to save enough to buy a day bed with lavender trim, a rainbow carpet to cover the lime green one that poked at the bottom of my feet, and a corner bar set (for non-alcoholic daiquiris). Realizing it would take forever, I came up with back-up plans: a day bed made from a mattress and pillows, using one of my mother's special carpets that were rolled up in a corner of the shed awaiting a day she'd have a place for them again, crafting the bar from a yard-sale table.

Through all the planning, my mother never said no. She wouldn't kill the dream. She asked how I'd do my homework and how I'd deal with the spider crickets (I'd woken her up in the middle of the night frantic after one jumped two feet in the air across our bedroom and I'd frequently made the excuse that I couldn't retrieve items from the shed because of the bugs). I could do my homework in the living room, and I was somehow convinced the crickets would be repelled by my perfect vision.

I know now my mother was never going to let me move into a shed without insulation or heat, a room that wasn't waterproof enough to keep the rain and snow from seeping into the carpet from beneath the walls. But she listened. She leafed through the magazines with me and pointed out the blankets and pillows she thought would best match my sketches.

I went away one weekend. When I returned, I walked into the trailer toward the back to drop off my things, but stopped midway down the hall at my mother's bedroom. I wondered why my school certificate was now hanging on the wall just inside, and a curtain rod was hanging across the doorway (there'd been no door for the last four years we'd lived there). My mom and sister stood behind me.

The room still had my mother's bed, which took up most of the small space, except a thin strip of walkway between the bed and the wall, but the bed had a new blanket. Dried flowers were hung over the tiny window on the far wall. In the corner at the foot of the bed, my mother squeezed a narrow corner shelf, the knick-knacks and figurines I'd collected from yard sales arranged on each level. On the bottom shelf sat the ornate jar I'd bought at a flea market. My mother and sister spent all weekend moving my things into the bedroom. And they cleaned out the shed to make a place for my mother to sleep.

I was too thrilled at having my own room, and maybe too self-absorbed to realize that my mother had given up the space she needed to give me mine.

I spent the afternoon arranging my things in the few available spaces, imagining the decorations I would put on the wall and how I might fashion a desk over my bed. I didn't give a thought to my mother settling in the shed or how she would fare with the spider crickets, or the chill of the spring air at night. But I felt seen and heard, and I was able to be alone.

In that room, I practiced my borrowed piccolo, wrote stories and poems, made lists of places I wanted to see someday. It's the last place I remember feeling truly lost to my dreams.

My mother piled as many covers as she could on top of her bed in the winter and ran an extension cord into the trailer to power an electric blanket or a fan. When the roof started leaking, she paid more to patch it than the shed was probably worth. She'd sometimes call for us in the winter mornings to bring her robe so she could jump into it as soon as she pulled back the covers, staving off the bite of icy air. We knew to always keep the door open from the hallway to the shed to let as much air as possible into her room during the depths of winter cold and peaks of summer heat.

My mother slept in that shed until I left for college. She weathered the extremes, hoping with each shiver and swelter that she could press back enough on the unforgiving walls to bend the limits.

***

Brie Deyton's writing has appeared in River Teeth's *Beautiful Things*, Creative Nonfiction's *Sunday Short Reads*, and *South Florida Poetry Journal*. She is currently working on a novel.

10 | A Deaf Heart: They Hear with their Eyes by Dwayne A. Harris

At an early age, I wanted to learn sign language to communicate with my deaf brother Al, and his friend Harold. Al was eight years older than me. He was born hearing and became deaf at five months. He became ill with a high fever that affected his cochlear and lost his hearing. He was considered pre-lingually deaf.

I learned his history from my mother when I was an adult, but as a nine-year-old child I did not know why my brother was different from my seven other siblings. We would have family dinners where all the kids spoke at once and Al sat in silence. I knew he could not speak, and I finally asked, "Dad, why can't Al talk?"

"He was born that way." My father said, and that was it. No details.

I said to my father, "When I grow up, I will learn how to communicate with him."

I loved Al, but it was a silent love, which motivated me to connect with him even though I did not understand how to communicate with him.

The family communicated with Al through *home signs*, which are a kind of pantomime we used, but it wasn't actual sign language. Using home signs was typical for many families back in the 1970s and still is in some families today.

My brother learned sign language at the deaf school he attended. In those days, deaf kids were isolated in public schools without proper services because of their disability. And as I became a pre-teen, I wanted to learn sign language. I became passionate about it, secretly watching my brother and Harold sign so I could memorize certain gestures. I had no idea American Sign Language

(ASL) was a legitimate language, but I wanted to learn Black deaf ASL.

By watching Al and Harold, I was able to sign basic things such as, *how are you? My name is...* everyday communication.

Harold was a student in the deaf school with Al, and he lived in the neighborhood. Whenever Harold came by, my brother lit up. Harold treated me like I was his little brother too. When he came to the door, I would try my best to sign, and he would smile brightly. Harold was the first deaf person besides my brother I knew well. He had a kind demeanor and smiled often.

My brother and Harold slowly taught me sign language. But sign language in our community was negative because being deaf was a stigma. They would call deaf people things like, *deaf and dumb* or a *deaf mute*. Those negative stereotypes angered me because I didn't see the deaf community that way. When Al and Harold first introduced me to their community of deaf friends it was overwhelming but also exciting to watch the deaf sign to one another. I witnessed a language as beautiful as a butterfly with colorful wings flying through the trees. It was the beginning of a love affair with an entire Black deaf community based on my love for my brother. I was honored to be a part of their community. I was able to learn a new language that did not exist in the hearing world. It made me sad that sign language was not being supported and that the deaf community was seen as unworthy. I strongly believed this situation had to be addressed for this silent minority, as well as for my deaf family and friends. I wanted to give them a voice, even if it was my own.

Then Harold went missing. He stopped coming over, and when I went to his house, no one answered the door. Weeks went by. Every day when I left for school, I asked my father to save me the newspaper, because I had a bad feeling. After two weeks, I saw it in the Chicago Sun Times, the newspaper article titled, "Deaf-Mute Dies in Hospital." My brother and I were devastated.

We later learned more details of how Harold died. He was in a serious hit and run accident and was taken to the nearest hospital where they refused to get a sign language interpreter, so he was unable to communicate his injuries to them. As a result, Harold died. Harold's death made me realize that deaf people need to communicate in healthcare settings, and I wanted to make that happen. Finding out the truth about Harold's death solidified my need to learn ASL formally.

I told my parents I wanted to study sign language, but there was only one school, and it was too far away. So, I immersed myself in the deaf world. I went to their parties, had a deaf girlfriend, and I read every book I could find on sign language. My goal was to work in a hospital setting and help deaf people. I finally became confident enough to get certified as a professional sign-language interpreter. That is when I met Ms. England, an older white woman and professional interpreter for many years. She worked in courts and a few hospitals. I shared my goals with her, and she encouraged me, saying I would be the first Black, male interpreter to work in that area and that my services were badly needed.

When I was in my early twenties, I worked at Thresholds a group home for deaf and hard-of-hearing people as a community service case manager. I escorted deaf and hard-of-hearing clients to their appointments. I was heartbroken to learn I was the only person helping them at these places. As a deaf advocate, I was prohibited to sign with my deaf clients about their health issues in appointments with a physician. I repeatedly advocated that healthcare organizations have a sign-language interpreter, but my recommendations were ignored.

When the American with Disabilities Act was signed into law in 1990, all hospitals were mandated to provide interpreters for all non-English speaking patients, but they ignored deaf and hard-of-hearing communities mostly because there was no way to identify the deaf individuals needing communication services.

In 1993, I was offered an opportunity at the University of Illinois Chicago Hospital (UIC) as a patient representative. I felt it was a sign from Harold, and I took the job, working with a physician and a couple of his deaf patients. My time was split between working in the clinic and being a patient rep. I recommended policies and procedures for the entire institution and provided deaf-culture trainings to help the university comply with ADA guidelines for deaf patients. I felt the support of my brother in this endeavor, and it motivated me to help an entire Black deaf community whom I loved so much.

At UIC Hospital, I implemented the Hearing with Their Eyes Cards for my brother's deaf friends to pass out to the deaf community. Deaf patients would present these cards in the hospital during appointments and emergency situations. The cards were in a variety of fluorescent colors, and they read, *I am deaf! Contact The Deaf Access Program.* Each card had my name and phone number.

In 1995, I created the Deaf Access Program (DAP) to ensure deaf patients could communicate in healthcare settings. DAP continues to provide communication services for this underserved community. We also trained medical professionals about how our DAP services work and the importance of expediting patients entering the clinical and emergency services areas. DAP identified the high-risk areas for deaf patients and partnered with the deaf community, professional sign-language groups, as well as businesses and organizations. Many organizations referred their deaf clientele to our program for medical services. I was proud of this achievement and credit the Black deaf community for their support. They saw me as a Black male professional fighting for the human rights and equality for their community in healthcare.

DAP still exists after twenty-five years with high level services for deaf and hard-of-hearing. My promise and goals were greatly exceeded.

Eventually, I was recruited by another local hospital, and I moved the entire program there. I set it up, hired and trained personnel, implemented policies for the deaf community, set standards and guidelines for the emergency room, and for labor and delivery. We had hundreds of employees who interacted with over two thousand deaf and hard-of-hearing individuals over eight years.

Two years later, I discovered this was the hospital where Harold died. I know I should have felt good that they finally had the program they so desperately needed, but I did not. This hospital neglected Harold, and I could not work for them anymore. I left.

I am proud of DAP and the impact they had on a voiceless community. It all started as a desire to learn how to communicate with my deaf brother and his friend, and it grew into a program for the deaf who desperately needed a voice in healthcare settings.

They now have a voice.

***

My brother and I have always had a deep bond that remains to this day.

When our mother passed away in 2007, my brother was the first person I wanted to see after she died. My family made the arrangements for my mother's funeral, but they neglected to get a sign-language interpreter for the event. I was furious! I tried to confirm an independent interpreter to ensure my brother would have the ability to understand and grieve with the entire family but I was unsuccessful.

I could not allow my brother to attend our mother's funeral without a sign language interpreter. With a heavy heart, I stood next to my mother's casket and interpreted the entire service for him.

The tears rolled down my brother's cheeks as the preacher spoke about my mother's life and her love for her children and friends. I held back my own tears as the entire church watched me sign to my brother and his closest deaf friends who were there to support him. I wanted to ensure my brother received these important words about our mother. It was the most difficult thing I've ever done. My love for my brother has always been my life's work and will always remain so. Every time I see my brother's smile, my deaf heart smiles.

***

Dwayne A Harris was born in Chicago and grew up with a deaf brother. He always wanted to share his story and the way it motivated him to accomplish a mission of love for an entire deaf community.

While working in a homeless youth shelter during the height of Covid, Dwayne noticed that the ear loops on masks interfered with listening devices. This inspired him to create a Helgie mask, a non-ear looping mask designed for people with hearing aids and cochlear implants. He now holds three patents.

Dwayne is currently working on a full-length stage play about how important communication is for deaf and hard-of-hearing individuals of all ethnic backgrounds.

11 | The Umbrella of Love by Sandra Hager Eliason

The day was overcast, cool for June, but the sun peeked between the clouds. It was a short walk to the university's West Bank, where I headed for a Vietnam War protest march, wanting to do more than helplessly watch as my male peers were drafted and died. It was 1970, and having just turned twenty-one, I could vote and legally drink. My male friends were drafted at age eighteen without those rights.

People approached from all directions, and I spotted Barry as it began to rain. He and I briefly flirted the previous fall when we met in the fall play. He had a bit part, while I played the lead. I was attracted to his easy smile, iridescent blond curls, and the kindness that emanated from him. He was only eighteen but seemed interested in me despite the fact I was an "older woman." We lost contact as we immersed ourselves in our different classes and activities. Now he was here, and he had an umbrella.

"I know you," I said as I approached, smiling playfully.

"Hey, hi." He smiled and introduced his friend.

"Could I by any chance share your umbrella?" I asked as the rain increased.

He spread it over the two of us and explained to his friend how we met. The crowd slowly ushered us along to begin the seven-mile walk down University Avenue to the Capitol. We spent most of the walk flirting, only stopping to chant, "One, two, three, four, we don't want your stinkin' war," or to sing the Country Joe and the Fish Vietnam war song, that referenced going to war to die. Otherwise, we were unaware of the passing scenery or others in the crowd. We virtually ignored his friend, who had his own umbrella.

By the time we reached the summit leading to the Capitol building, our attraction was cemented. The ache in my feet and legs

61

was overcome by the awe of the view, as I looked down at the mass of moving people, all of whom believed as passionately as we did that this war had to end.

Our first date was in my apartment, where I cooked broiled steak with mushrooms, green salad, and watermelon for dessert. I didn't like watermelon but thought he might. It turned out he didn't like watermelon either. We laughed at this commonality, and as he left, his soft lips brushed mine. I closed the door and rested my back against it, smiling.

As I turned to clean up, the sudden downpour of rain pelted the windows, with a flash of lightning and immediate boom of thunder. Barry was walking home, and this time he had no umbrella. I got into my car to look for him, drove up and down several streets, but somehow missed him. He had taken shelter in a gas station. I headed back home disappointed and worried.

He called when he got back to his room to say he was safe. I held the princess phone to my ear as I swooned onto the bed, imagining him on his bed. We decided we would always talk in the rain.

Barry and I saw each other regularly during the rest of the summer, our connection deepening. He worked as a night operator at a funeral home, and he sneaked me in after hours, when the home was dark and quiet. He would open the back door and lead me up the stairs to his small, cramped room with a bed, desk, and a hot plate for cooking. One night, there was a corpse on a gurney in the hall. I shivered, hurrying past.

As we laid on his bed and talked, I waited for the magic moment when a kiss would lead to more, and eventually, it did. When fall came, he officially moved into the dorm, although in reality he stayed with me every night, in the upper floor of a duplex the college owned. When it rained, we spread his old sleeping bag in the front hall under the eaves, cuddling in the dark and whispering, "I love you."

Eventually he abandoned his dorm and moved in with me. While Barry was back in classes, I took a job as a waitress at a bar close to our duplex. He worked as a cook at the college grill, but he showed up every night at 1:00 a.m., whether he had class in the morning or not. He walked me home through the dark streets to assure my safety.

Our living arrangement was a secret from his parents, who were paying for his campus room and board. I told mine in a letter, as an act of defiance. I had graduated from college and no longer owed obeisance to their old-fashioned ideas of morality.

Barry's parents didn't like the idea of my "cradle robbing," and blamed my bad influence for his lengthening hair, ripped jeans (which I lovingly patched), and newly found belief that war was wrong. The proper son they raised, educated in a conservative Lutheran school where dancing led to immorality, would not be involved in any of these things. And he certainly would not live with a girl before marriage.

Barry's parents discovered our living arrangement when they called his house with news of his grandfather's death. His roommate had been given strict instructions to lie about his whereabouts, but another housemate answered and said Barry was probably at my place, where he was staying. His parents were livid. They were paying for housing he was not using, never mind his unthinkable behavior. They gave him an ultimatum: end the relationship or they would no longer support him.

We were in love. We went everywhere together. I met his college friends, and we often sat around as he played guitar, singing folk songs. Our lives had integrated. We were invested in each other and the power of our beliefs. He would not leave me, he told them, and they cut him off.

Then we received a notice that our duplex was going to be demolished to make way for a dorm, and we had to move. We were living together illegally because college housing was segregated by sex. The only place we could move on campus was married student housing, which required us to be married.

Coincidentally, a letter arrived from my mother, who was embarrassed by our living situation. "Just tell us you're married," it said.

We had discussed marriage, but I was only twenty-two, and he not quite nineteen. We didn't want to give the state power to dictate our legal status. Marriage also meant I would have to give up my identity, becoming Mrs. Him. It was not until 1975 that women were legally allowed to keep their maiden name after marriage in Minnesota.

"My mother just wants to be able to tell people we're married, to justify our status," I told Barry. "What if we just do that?"

He thought a moment. "What do you mean, just say it?"

"What if we hold a commitment ceremony? Not a legal marriage, but a marriage in our hearts?"

"How would that work?" he asked.

"Create our vows and invite people to witness them."

"I guess we could do that," he said thoughtfully.

"Then we could tell people we were married but owe nothing to the state."

He nodded slowly, "Okay."

We set a date and invited a few friends to our living room. I made a long empire-waisted dress of flowered chiffon. He wore a brocade shirt. Our friends sat in a circle around us on the floor witnessing the words we spoke, affirming our love, and vowing commitment to one another. We believed in the power of our words and ideals, and believed speaking them would make them last.

After the ceremony, we felt safe telling campus housing we were married, and they accepted our word—as did my parents, who chose not to ask too many questions. His parents, however, were not moved. But we did not waver. We lived in campus housing until he graduated, then married legally in a small ceremony.

The Vietnam war eventually ended, the draft went away, and time passed. I completed more education and became a doctor. Barry continued to stand by me, working to support us while I was in medical school and residency, always sharing his half of the housework, and taking over primary childcare duties for our eventual three children when I was on call or tied up at the hospital. We recently celebrated our fiftieth wedding anniversary with our children and grandchildren around us. My three girls are proud to tell stories of how their father took on the traditional "mother" role while I went through medical training and practiced.

Looking back, I marvel at the kind of man so confident in his masculinity that he supported me as I reached for my dreams. I fear that lucky umbrella, the key to finding each other so long ago, is no longer with us. Its consequences, however, remain.

***

Sandra Hager Eliason is a retired Family Medicine doctor who is now writing full time. She graduated with a degree in English and Speech from Augsburg College (now Augsburg University) in Minneapolis before entering the University of North Dakota Medical School. She did her residency in Family Medicine at the University of Minnesota. Eliason practiced medicine for more than thirty years. In 2016, she won the Minnesota Medicine Magazine Arts Edition writing contest. Since then, she has been published in Bluestem magazine, West Trade Review, the Brevity blog three times, been anthologized in the e-book Tales From Six Feet Apart, and Pure Slush, vol. 23. She has an upcoming piece in The Linden Review. She is a book reviewer for Hippocampus Magazine and has published reviews in the Brevity Blog and Rain Taxi. She resides with her husband in Minneapolis, Minnesota where she tends a garden in the summer and has a cat to warm her lap in the winter. She is on twitter @SandraHEliason1 and Instagram @sheliasonmd.

12 | Marrow by Tania Richard

Hi Love of my life,
Make the best of every day!
Be happy.
Reach for the stars.
God bless you!
—Mama!

My mother sent me this note through the mail years ago while I was living in Chicago. I don't remember the reason. Perhaps she was giving me a pep talk. I framed it and put it on a shelf in my bedroom.

My mother was my biggest fan and didn't believe in nerves. She was an accomplished woman, valedictorian of her medical school, a beloved gynecologist. When I was nervous before an audition or performance, she admonished me in her Haitian trill, "Why would you be nervous? Aren't you doing what you want to do?"

"Well, yeah," I'd answer.

"Then why waste your time with nerves?"

Her logic made sense so there was no point in holding on to my anxiety.

When I played the character Mame in my senior year of high school, my mother saw every performance. She was happy to stand in the corner of the gym if there weren't any tickets. She gave me a white dress from her closet that still had the tags on it because she didn't like the costume they gave me.

"You have such a presence, Tania. All the lights shine on you," she would say. And while my father dismissed my acting in plays as a hobby, she lifted me up to my destiny.

In sixth grade, I came home after school with a four-alarm emergency, "I have to get a Mother Karen jacket. Everyone has one, and I must have one too."

I was obsessed because all the white girls wore them, including the most popular one, Tricia. She was the first to wear a Mother Karen jacket. Each day more girls came to school wearing them. The color blocked outerwear was a pullover. The sleeves were a primary color and the material that covered the torso was a complimentary primary color. The front of the jacket had a big pocket where you could carry things middle school girls carried around with them. Perhaps it was where those cool girls carried their "coolness." The jacket had a zipper above the pocket and the rim of the jacket and collar were the same color as the sleeves. Mother Karens were worn by everyone cool. The only people who didn't wear them were obviously losers.

My mother was at the kitchen sink when I made my proclamation about the need for the jacket. I didn't even say hello first. She stopped what she was doing, grabbed her purse and took me to a store to buy one. No questions asked. She didn't always do what I wanted her to do the minute I asked. But when she sensed a deep need buried in something superficial, she answered the call.

She was no pushover, though, and there were some non-negotiables. For example, she never wanted me to get in cars with friends. When I was in college, she insisted I take the bus rather than ride with my friend Gary. His parents lived in the neighborhood closest to ours. It was much easier to get a ride with him. Plus, I was secretly in love with him, so a two-hour drive was a chance to have him all to myself.

I didn't tell my mother that. Instead, I screamed over the phone and threatened not to come home, even though I didn't mean it. I craved my father's made-to-order dinners like Chicken Clemençeau. I yearned for evenings watching *Touched by an Angel* as my mother sat in the reclining chair doing her crossword and eating chocolate kisses.

My mother didn't want me taking long rides because she was afraid I'd get in a car accident. Short distances with friends were somehow fine. It didn't matter that a bus could just as easily get into an accident. Forbidding rides with friends in cars for long distances was how she tried to ensure my safety.

She lost her mother when she was seven years old. Odeide Leon died while giving birth to my mother's brother. Her father sent her and six siblings to live with relatives while he remarried and had more children, whom she never met.

In 1990, my older sister Lissa was killed in a car accident. She was only twenty-one years old when she took a ride from a friend. Lissa decided at the last minute to hop in and join a friend for a brief run to the store. The short distance didn't protect her. She was killed instantly when an eighteen-year-old drunk driver hit her side of the car.

I sat in the stairwell of our home as my mother spoke on the phone. A technician from the morgue called to confirm Lissa's death. Her worst fear of losing a child in a car accident had come true, and that taught me to expect the worst-case scenario in all situations moving forward.

Before my sister's funeral, my mother visited the church bathroom for at least twenty minutes. She was sick to her stomach with grief. I sat in the lobby waiting for her. I was anxious because if she was having a bowel movement, the single stall would smell afterwards. From a young age, my mother insisted the smell of a bowel movement had to be covered with air freshener immediately. I was stressed because there was no air freshener available. She exited the bathroom and took two or three steps away from the open door. I smiled trying to convey, *It's okay. Don't worry. It's okay.*

"Je ne me sans pas bien," she said apologetically, which means "I don't feel well." On the worst day of her life, she was laid bare, and there was nothing I could do to save her.

My mother always remembered me even as she struggled with dementia. And when she lay in the emergency room unconscious from a stroke, she squeezed my hand when I tried to let hers go. The hospice worker stopped by with materials to start the transition from nursing home to hospice care.

The doctor told me it could be months before she passed. I spent the day in her hospital room skimming through magazines rather than talking to her, thanking her, and comforting her. I thought I had more time. I slept at home that night because I believed she would be around for months. I've since learned that doctors pad the amount of time they think a patient has left as a source of comfort. It's easier than telling a broken-hearted family member the truth. She died early the next morning. It was a sucker punch followed by a right hook. The sting has never gone away.

At the funeral home, they asked whether I wanted to see her one more time before cremation. When my father died, the funeral director encouraged me to see the body as a means of closure. It did not provide closure. I would not make the same mistake with her. It was hard enough that the last image I have of her, she is lying in the hospital bed; head tilted to the side with tubes in her nose.

One final photograph is a selfie I took of us at the nursing home when I last saw her alive. We are arm in arm. The image is mostly a blur, but you can see we are smiling. That is the picture I hang onto.

Six months after I got married, I stood in church with my mother as my stepchildren lined up for their first communion. "It's been six months," she sang as she handed me a brown paper bag filled with a bottle of folic acid pills. She walked away and joined my father sitting in a pew.

Folic acid is a vitamin women can take in preparation for pregnancy. My mother never mentioned children to me. She never asked if I wanted to have children or if we were trying. It was a fait accompli in her mind and the bag of folic acid was the starter pistol.

For years I denied that I wanted to be a mother even though a cute baby would stop me in my tracks. I listed all the reasons why I didn't want to have kids: Reason #365: They're expensive. Reason # 202: They suck the life out of ya. In truth I was protecting myself. I didn't date much in my late twenties and thirties. I never thought I'd get married. And I had no desire to have children on my own. So, I suppressed any maternal yearning as a means of protection. I started taking the folic acid the next day and got pregnant on our first try.

My mother loved babies. I've inherited that love and wish I could walk around with a pin that says, "baby whisperer." This pin would let new mothers know they can pass their baby off to me in public and I will hold them while they finish shopping or whatever they need to do. When I hear a baby cry, it takes restraint for me not to follow the sound and try to comfort them. My mother use to give newborns a quick squeeze and kiss on the forehead before she passed them to the delivery nurse. She was their first burst of love.

My mother had fair skin and jet-black hair like the singer Lena Horne, and a nose that lives on my daughter Odeide's face. I have a black and white photo of her at fifteen that could be a picture of my child, who is currently fifteen. My kid rolls her eyes whenever I tease her about the similarity and say, "Stop looking exactly like my mother," or "Oh my gosh, that was so my mom." She rolls her eyes with upturned lips, a not so concealed smile.

My mother thought Odeide was remarkable. "She *co-nnects* with people. She is *spe-cial*," she'd marvel.

I have a running joke that my parenting is based solely on not giving my kids fodder for a future therapist's couch. It's an impossible goal.

Still, in all my years of therapy I never focused on my mother, imperfect as she was. It's because I never doubted that she loved me. She thought I was the moon and stars.

I would catch her sometimes watching me. We'd be sitting at the kitchen table or hanging out in her bedroom, and I could see her in my periphery looking my way. Rather than look back and break her gaze I'd stay in position and let her marvel at what she created. I was there because of her, and she had every right to admire her work, imperfect as I was.

Now I do the same with my daughters who both look like her. One is more similar to her than the other, but there is no mistaking from where they came. And every time I parent well and love them from my marrow, I remember where I came from as well.

***

Tania Richard is a published writer, award-winning actress, teacher, and antiracism educator. Her platform, Tania's Take race, culture and the culture of race, showcases her podcast, essays, educational content, and videos. Her blog, *Writing My Mind* was on The Chicago Tribune's blog site for ten years. Her books are *My So-Called Unexpected Life; The 10 Things I Did to Meet and Marry My Man, Be A Stepmom, Have Babies & Embrace the Life I Never Knew I Wanted,* and *Unexpected Life: Interviews About Embracing the Unexpected* (Amazon). She's also an award-winning playwright. Her commentary can be heard on OUT Chicago, NPR's The Story, All Things Considered and WTTW's Chicago Tonight. As an actress, she has appeared on Chicago Fire, Chicago Justice, Chicago PD, Empire, and in national commercials for Lowes and BMO Harris among others. She has performed on Broadway, with Steppenwolf Theatre Company, The Goodman Theatre, The Second City, and other theatres.

13 | Rachel (Not) Getting Married by Claude Clayton Smith

We were twenty when we met sophomore year in The Philosophy of Education class. Then we played tennis. Afterward, we took an elevator to the top of the science building. The new science building was going to be eight stories high, but they had only completed the first seven. The eighth was still under construction. But the elevator went all the way to the top, where an expanse of bare concrete awaited the installation of heavy-duty industrial carpeting scattered in rolls all over the place. The hallways, lacking wallboard, were framed with two by fours and strung with heavy BX cable. Overhead, plastic pipes ran through a maze of crisscrossed wire struts from which the ceiling tile would eventually be dropped. They had not yet put in several windows, so a cool breeze filtered throughout the vast open space, delicious to anyone who had just been playing tennis, which we had.

What followed was one of those beautiful moments in which two people realize they have a connection, established of its own sweet accord. A few hours earlier we had merely been classmates, wrestling with Alfred North Whitehead, but now we were wrestling with the recognition that we were alone in this unfinished space, a space that (like what was about to happen) was pure potential. Rachel was much shorter than I, until she stood rather playfully on a length of rolled-up carpeting, bringing us face to face, her curly hair a delightful tangle, her soft dark eyes gleaming. Our tennis sweat had dried by then, the cool breeze had turned a trifle chilly, and so we leaned toward each other naturally, just for the warmth of it. Soon my arms slipped around her waist, and we embraced. Then we kissed, and that did it.

"I'm Jewish," Rachel warned, after the third kiss.

"I don't care," I said. I was hell bent for Hadassah.

We were twenty-two, seniors in college, when we made plans to get married. But I was half-Catholic (my father was the grandson of a Methodist minister) and Rachel was all-Jewish. So her parents made me invisible. The half and the whole just didn't add up. Rachel's father was a university math professor who'd written a textbook with many esoteric equations, but in none of them did one-half Catholic = Jewish.

My friend, Ed Schwartz, a fellow student in our teacher education program, was Jewish, and as he explained when I took up Judaism, "I don't care what you do, you can never be a M-O-T."

"*M-O-T?*" I wasn't Jewish, just a wannabe, so I asked the obvious: "What's the good word?" I thought he'd lapsed into French, as in *bon mot.*

"Member of the tribe."

"Wouldn't that be M-O-T-T? Like the apple juice?"

"Call it what you will," Ed retorted. "You can never belong."

He was right, of course, but I was young, and as Hemingway once put it, you do things because you're young and don't know any better. So why *couldn't* half a Catholic marry a whole Jew? Well, I was going to find out.

Rachel could hold her own on the tennis court, where my performance—given that I'd come to college with a tennis racquet purchased with Green Stamps—did little for our "love match." But I experienced a moment of glory in my own sport that year, which helped cement our relationship. A group of teachers from the big inner-city high school, where we were logging our observation hours, wanted to challenge the basketball varsity team, which annually made a run for the state title. They created a charity event, which would pack the gym to the rafters. One teacher had played on a foreign Olympic team, and when he learned I played for the university, he asked me to join them. He was the star, and I would play a supporting role. But when the game was tied in the last seconds, he was double-teamed and the ball came to me for a little hook shot I banked right in, bringing us the win as the buzzer sounded. But all I cared about at the time was that Rachel was watching. And when that little hook shot went in, I looked to find her in the stands, where her soft dark eyes were gleaming brighter than ever at her would-be Jew.

In February of our senior year, Rachel gave me a large poster-board with a question mark in the center for Valentine's Day. She peppered the board with a list of options for the future—things I'd talked about doing before I'd met her: *Live with Gramps and write the Great American Novel. Go to medical school. Go to divinity school. Join the Peace Corps.* We celebrated the day with a bottle of wine in front of the fireplace in my dorm room. I'm embarrassed to admit that Rachel and I were virgins. She was a good Jewish girl, and my mother's Catholic half of my religious upbringing had kept my urges in check. But I hoped that this would be "the night."

Unfortunately, the fireplace in my dorm room didn't work. It hadn't been cleaned in years, didn't draw well, and no one bothered to tell me. Rachel and I were sprawled on a blanket in front of the fire when I excused myself to go to the men's room. As I stepped into the hallway, I found it choked with smoke. We hadn't noticed it because smoke rises, and we'd been on the floor. Throwing open the windows, we quickly smothered the flames—a symbolic moment, in retrospect—and joined the student exodus to await the fire department.

Undaunted, I hung that question mark on my dorm room wall while Rachel and I continued our forbidden love. This secret was one we shared with fellow students and Rachel's kid sister Ina, who came to campus for a visit one weekend and promised not to tell.

After graduation, Rachel accepted a teaching job near her home in Chicago. Then, without telling her parents, came to meet *my* parents in Connecticut. Ironically, in an old issue of *National Geographic*, I'd found a story on the land of Israel, complete with glossy desert photographs and a text that made the history of the Jews both romantic and exciting. I'd cut out one photograph and hung it on my bedroom wall, a bloody sun that could have been rising or setting over an immense sand dune.

The visit went swimmingly. Rachel and I escaped to Long Island Sound, to one of those sandy stretches where cattails rise along the shore, providing total privacy to any couple on a blanket—except from overhead, where small aircraft were circling to land at an airport nearby. They came in lower and lower as if to check us out, as the temperature got higher and higher on that blanket below. But if we looked up, there was nothing but the glare of the sun. So, we kept on hugging and kissing. Before long, Rachel rolled on top of me and suddenly my groin exploded in a moment of sun-splashed ecstasy. Chagrined, I rolled over to conceal the stain in my shorts, leaving Rachel unaware of what had happened.

In September, Rachel moved to Chicago for her teaching job, and I accepted a teaching/coaching job in the D.C. area. I promised her I would visit once we were both settled so we could break our news to her parents. But suddenly Rachel telephoned to say she was coming to visit me.

"We have to talk," she said. She sounded shell-shocked, and it was because her period was late. She'd gone forty days without her period. Forty days and forty nights. It sounded biblical, threatening to punctuate our relationship with an exclamation point. She said she'd fly in that very weekend. Could I fetch her at the airport? I went to the airport expecting to drive her to my new apartment, but she carried no luggage. She was catching a return flight home that very evening. We had to talk in the terminal.

"Ina squealed," she said abruptly, stepping from the jetway. There was no hug or kiss, just a blank look on her face.

"Double trouble," I muttered. I now knew the photograph of the sun I'd cut from *National Geographic* was setting.

"How could I be pregnant?" Rachel exclaimed. "I'm a virgin!"

The way she said it left no doubt that it was true.

I had a confession to make, good half-Catholic, that I was, "When we were at the beach, Rachel, I—"

We ducked out of the stream of disembarking passengers and took seats in an empty lounge.

"Well?" Rachel's dark eyes were waiting, her face framed by soft curls. In the pain of our predicament, she'd never looked more beautiful.

"When you were on top of me at the beach, I—I *came*."

"Ejaculated?" she asked.

I nodded.

"But you had your shorts on. Me too!"

"It was quite a load."

"Do you know the *odds* against that?"

"You're the math teacher." I was thinking of her father's textbook with all of its crazy equations.

"Do your parents know about your period?"

"They only know about you."

"And that's enough, I suppose."

"The only thing worse than a Jew with no sons, is a Jew with a *goy* for a son-in-law. They've forbidden me to see you again," she said with a down-turned face.

"But you're here."

"I told my parents I couldn't leave you without seeing you."

"You're *leaving* me?"

"I promised."

"And if you're pregnant?"

She had no answer for that, and neither did I.

Then came the long, dark, lonely ride back to my apartment, during which a sense of depression overwhelmed me as I drove. It was a feeling unlike any I'd ever known.

But that depression lifted four days later (day forty-eight) when Rachel called to say that her period had begun. I guess that bloody sun was rising after all.

"That's … wonderful," I said.

There was a long pause. I think Rachel was crying. Then she said goodbye and wished me a good life.

Which, eventually, would come to pass.

***

Claude Clayton Smith has an MFA in fiction from the University of Iowa's Writers' Workshop. He wrote a novel for his DA dissertation at Carnegie-Mellon. He also holds an MAT from Yale and a BA from Wesleyan (CT).

Claude's story, *Helping Padraig Die* won the 2021 Great Midwest Fiction Contest of the *Midwest Review*. Most recently, he was a finalist for the 2022 First Pages Prize and Driftwood Press short story award.

He is the author of a novel, *The Stratford Devil*; four books of creative nonfiction (*Ohio Outback, Lapping America, Red Men in Red Square, and Quarter-Acre of Heartache*); two Little Golden Books (*The Cow and the Elephant* and *The Gull That Lost the Sea*); and a volume of poetry (Sonnets & Such). Four of his plays have been awarded full production in competition.

Claude served as joint editor/translator of four books of Native Siberian Literature, earning him a medal from the United Nations citing him as a "Friend of Native Peoples." His own books have been translated into five languages, including Russian and Chinese.

A Professor Emeritus of English at Ohio Northern University, he lives with his wife of forty-six years in Madison, Wisconsin.

His website is: claudeclaytonsmith.wordpress.com.

14 | That Time We Didn't Die in a Grill Fire by Jaclyn Hamer

When we pull into my aunt's driveway, one of my cousins is standing in the front yard holding a barking dog and a baby we haven't met yet. Neither belong to her.

"The grill's on fire," she says, wild-eyed, gesturing toward the house. "Like, it's covered in flames, and they won't leave."

That no one else is heeding the danger does not surprise me. We've never been a group for taking the rational route.

"Stay here," my dad yells as he dashes towards the front door. Cousin, dog, baby, and I watch him charge up the steps and fall, smashing his knee into the brick. He stands, looks at the blood dripping down his leg, and continues inside with a small limp.

My cousin leans in to hug me and the new baby drools on my neck. "Hey Jac."

It's been over a year since we were all together at Grandma's funeral. I hate the idea of gathering without her—of not being enveloped in softness and Shalimar the second I walk through the door. She taught us that earthworms were great for gardens, that parents' punishments didn't apply at her house, that more dessert was always a good idea, and that there's nothing more magical than a dragonfly landing on an outstretched finger. She was warmth, kindness, and comfort—the one who kept us all together. I don't know how we'll function as a group without her. Can a family still be a family without its center? My answer just might lie in the fact that the entire group has placed themselves in mortal peril and no one is trying to do much about it.

I follow my dad into the house but stop in the kitchen while he continues to the back porch toward the burning grill. My aunt is yelling for someone's boyfriend, who is apparently asleep in the basement, while two of my cousins are in a screaming match over the landline telephone.

"Get out of the house," one cousin shrieks.

"I'm talking to 911!" the other one snaps back, stretching the phone cord from the wall to keep it out of her sister's grasp. Cousin One concedes and heads out the back door to try and convince someone else to get away from the danger.

"Oh, hey Jac," Cousin Two says, leaning in for a hug and rolling her eyes. "Eleven people running around screaming about a fire, and I'm the only one who thought the fire department should be involved."

Looking out through the kitchen window, I can see the grill ensconced in three-foot flames. They're waving in the air above the open lid and crawling down the back towards the house. It's a wonder the porch hasn't caught on fire yet. The kitchen is already hazy with smoke and about twenty degrees hotter than it should be.

Grandma's hummingbird feeder hangs about four feet from the grill. It hasn't had a visitor since my aunt brought it here after the funeral. Although everyone's been telling her to get rid of it, I can see that she's filled it to the brim with jewel-red nectar. I'm with her. Giving up on Grandma's hummingbirds feels like saying goodbye all over again. I have an urge to move it to safety, but the chaos on the back porch doesn't need another body.

"What the hell are you still doing in here? Are you seriously on the phone?" My uncle says to my cousin as he charges in through the back door and yells for everyone to go out front.

"Oh, hey Jac." He leans in for a hug and then resumes calling us all idiots for staying in the house. My cousin yells back that if it's so dumb, he should leave too.

"Get off the damn phone!" he says, and heads back to the inferno.

I wonder what Grandma would think of us, running around like lunatics and screaming at each other in the name of love. Scared for our lives, but even more terrified of losing someone else, we hover in place while begging everyone else to leave.

The fire is taller than the window now, and I can hear Dad yelling and my aunt sobbing over the crackle of the flames. Grandpa shuffles into the kitchen with a one-ounce paper Dixie cup. He holds it to the water dispenser in the fridge and waits patiently while it fills at a glacial pace. He carries it even more slowly out the back door so as not to spill a single drop. A minute later, he is back at the refrigerator for a refill.

"You guys really should get out of the house," another aunt says while she stands there watching him, transfixed like the rest of us.

Out back, the grill is a spectacle of light. All eyes are on the flames crawling down the propane tube towards the tank, which will surely blow at any second.

"Everyone needs to get into the front yard," my father says with an authority that no one heeds.

My aunt won't abandon the house she loves, her children won't leave her behind, my grandfather thinks he's saving the day, and my dad thinks he's responsible for all of them. My aunt wails. Everyone yells:

"The flames are really close to the tank."

"It's gonna blow."

"Go out front!"

"I'm going to lose my house."

"Better than your life!"

My cousin comes to the door with the phone in the crook of her neck. "The fire department says to get away from the grill and go wait in the front yard."

No one cares.

We can barely hear the sirens over the blazing fire, the tears, and all the opinions. The firefighters have to physically drag my aunt and her entourage from the back porch to the driveway. The flames are tamed, and as my aunt stifles her tears, she sees me and leans in for a hug. "Oh, hey Jac."

We're all together in the driveway, laughing and hugging and already thinking about the years we'll spend telling this story. The firefighters tell us what a close call we had, but we're too giddy to hear it.

We're fine. We are together, and we are fine.

As we joke, a brilliant green and pink hummingbird flutters at the feeder. Hovering above us, it drinks in the sweet, fire-warmed nectar.

***

Jaclyn Hamer is an advertising copywriter, a member of Women's Fiction Writers Association (WFWA), and a champion of the Oxford comma. Her stories have appeared in *Fearsome Critters*, *The Bookends Review*, and *The Bookends Review Best of 2019* print anthology. When she's not writing, she can be found hanging with her daughter and three rescue cats, trying to convince her husband they need more animals.

15 | The Love of My Life by Nadia Felecan

I quietly knocked on the door of my father's study. I put my ear to the door to catch any sounds but heard nothing. Was this a good time to disturb him? Was he grading papers? Was he reading? I knocked a little louder. My all-A report card in my hand gave me the courage: I would only be a minute. I wanted to show him my grades so he would be proud of me. Plus, I was going to ask him to sign it and show my classmates his signature. Everyone knew my father: he was the handsome genius, the dean of the main university in town. To have his signature on my report card was something I had been dreaming of for a while.

After I knocked again, I heard his voice with a bit of irritation, "Just come in."

As I walked in, careful not to make too much noise, he barked at me without lifting his head from the book he was reading, "What do you want?"

I could not speak for what seemed like several minutes. All I could do was give him my report card with a shaky hand. He grabbed it, looked at it bored, and gave it back to me saying, "You are in elementary school; you'd better only have A's. Show me your report card when you are in high school. Now, leave me alone, go have your mother sign it, and stop wasting my time with this nonsense."

I turned around feeling relieved that he didn't get more upset and walked quickly out of his study before he threw something after me. All I wanted was for him to be proud of me.

A couple of years later, in 7th grade, I had that same sinking feeling when my French teacher called my name again. I stood by my desk waiting for her to quiz me about yesterday's lesson, which I did not review. She called on me the day before, so I wondered why she would quiz me two days in a row. My voice shook despite giving the correct answer for every question, and she gave me 100 percent on the oral quiz.

She exclaimed, "Nadia, I am so proud of you. You impress me. I quizzed you yesterday, and I thought, I'd quiz you again today. You were prepared both days. Good job!"

I was surprised. She was proud of me! I've never had anybody say they were proud of me. I cried and explained that she should not be proud because I did not study. I just had a good memory and tried hard to remember what she taught. She winked at me through her thick glasses, smiled with her bright red lipstick-covered lips, and said that she was even more proud.

After that day, I worked hard to learn French. I wanted her to continue to be proud of me. I went to the library, got books in French, and wrote and memorized lists of new vocabulary. She taught us basic French grammar in class, but I taught myself how to conjugate difficult verbs. While my classmates were trying to form a question, I was ready to converse in French. I checked in with my teacher, stayed after school, and asked for recommendations to learn more French.

I looked forward to my time with her because sometimes she would give me gifts. One time she gave me a bookmark with the Eiffel Tower on it, another time she presented me with a Larousse dictionary, which was the best French dictionary. On another occasion, she gave me a book in French that I read nightly. She made me feel valued. She commented on my enthusiasm and determination to learn a new language.

Although she didn't have any children, she told me she would have wanted me as her child. I dreamt of having her as my mother. This woman in her late 30s, tall and slender, always with a smile and words of praise and encouragement, could have been my mother! I imagined being her only child and receiving gifts of French books from her. I would not feel anxious every time I went home, wondering if my father would hit my mom, my siblings, or me. I would not have to lie at school and say that my bruises and welts were from falling, or from little scuffles with my brothers. My life would be perfect if only I could be her daughter.

I poured myself into studying French even more. Our after-school meetings were full of enjoyable conversations, laughter, and sometimes she hugged me when I left. We read scenes from classic French books like *Les Misérables*. We took turns reading Moliere's plays and getting silly with our voices. I lived for those moments with her. I lived for that occasional hug because that was the only time when I felt loved.

One day, she asked me if I wanted to learn to play the piano. Of course I did. I would do anything to make her proud of me. She said the piano teacher was coming to school the next day and I could start my first lesson in our after-school meeting. I was elated.

The next day, she reminded me about the piano lesson. She gave me a smile and assured me I would do well. The rest of the classes that day were just a blur. My heart was jumpy with excitement. I fixed my eyes on the classroom clock as I impatiently counted the hours and minutes until 4 o'clock. When the final bell rang, I jumped off my seat, ready to run to her office.

But before I got a chance, the principal walked into our classroom and told us she had an important announcement. As she opened her mouth, tears started trickling down her cheeks.

"Your French teacher... she had a heart attack this afternoon. She died. Don't come to your first-period class tomorrow because we don't have a sub yet."

I couldn't breathe. I felt like I had been punched in the stomach, and I was frozen. I could not cry or scream. An avalanche of "no mores" flooded my brain, drowning me in a sea of darkness.

No piano class. No more French after-school meetings. No more hugs. No more love.

My world lost its guiding light and crumbled. My French teacher was gone, but I was not done making her proud. The following year, I took the entrance exam to study French at a foreign-language high school. Every time I needed some words of encouragement, or when things at home got violent, I visited my elementary-school hallways and looked at her pictures on the walls. I would whisper to her, "I am going to be a French teacher like you. I will never disappoint you."

After moving to the United States, I continued my studies and became a French teacher, carrying her legacy and sharing love and words of praise and encouragement with my students. Every time I plan a French lesson, every time I enter the classroom, I strive to create a learning environment for my students, like my French teacher did for me. I want my students to experience a place full of love, encouragement, laughter, and acceptance. I know that some of my students struggle in their lives, and I want to be for them what my French teacher was for me: a beacon of love, hope, and positivity. My French teacher sensed my need for love, but she never knew the details of my family life, and looking back, she was the guiding light I needed. She showed me that I mattered. She showed me the world has love in it, and that it has adults who can be trusted.

***

Nadia Felecan grew up in Romania, Transylvania. Born in 1976, the year when Nadia Comaneci earned the first-ever perfect score in gymnastics, she was named in her honor. However, Nadia Felecan is one of the least coordinated people (just go out dancing with her)!

At the age of twenty-one, she moved to Chicago where she earned a bachelor's degree in French and two master's degrees: one in Special Education and one in Linguistics. She is a fluent speaker of four languages: Romanian, French, English, and Spanish.

In 2022, she was awarded an English language fellowship to teach English in Baku, Azerbaijan. A mother of three boys and two cats, she is a teacher by day and strives to become a storyteller by night. She has been telling her stories at the Story Lab, Pour One Out, The Moth, and Soul Stories. She loves cake and motorcycles equally.

16 | Improvising My Way through Loss by Ellen Birkett Morris

Comedy is an escape, not from truth but from despair, a narrow escape into faith.
~Christopher Fry, English poet and playwright

It was easy to imagine that everything was normal. My mom was in her rocking chair. The television played reruns of The Waltons. It could have been the 1970s. I could have been eight and crawling onto her lap for her all-encompassing, warming hugs. But it was 2016, and our conversation was punctuated by her fits of coughing. I watched as her body shook, my fear increasing. She coughed, and choked, and when it was over, she looked at me and wryly said, "Don't panic."

My cool, funny mom was diagnosed with stage-four lung cancer. As a retired nurse, she believed in faith and medicine. There must be something to faith. When I was born three-months prematurely in 1965, Mom made sure I had a good doctor *and* got all the Jesuit brothers at a seminary in Milford, Ohio to pray for me. I made it.

Mom was always my greatest cheerleader. She never failed to encourage me as I joined the school paper, wrote my first professional articles (all of which she mailed to her older sister), or published my first essay.

I can still see the pride shining through her expression on my wedding day. Her little girl, who almost didn't make it, had found love. She reveled in the joy of my strong relationship with my husband and said she couldn't have picked a better mate for me.

Mom's house was the site of many family feasts. During these dinners, I would look over at her as she watched the family she created enjoying each other's company. She was the heart of our family. I knew that the world would be a less welcoming place without her.

My goal now was not to sink under the weight of my sadness at her illness, so I could be present for whatever moments we could share. I wanted to offer her at least a small portion of the encouragement and love she had offered me.

My mom tried multiple treatments but couldn't catch a break. I watched as she got weaker. I'd sit with her in doctor's offices, hoping upon hope, but the cancer spread, and her options narrowed.

I tried hard to keep the faith, but I could feel her slipping away. Feeling empty and numb, I needed something to make me come alive and offer a temporary diversion from the horror of the impending loss of my mother. Some people look to sex, alcohol, or drugs. I signed up for an improvisation class.

I'd often read my writing in public, but improv was something entirely different. There was no script. No created world. I'd have to react to others on the fly. The prospect was terrifying.

The class was in an old chapel with pews for seats. Our jovial hosts punctured the solemnity with funny introductions of themselves, while we tense students laughed nervously. There were four of us, led by a mellow teacher with an unlikely name, Chris Anger.

Chris gave us gentle guidelines. "Don't try to be funny. Say yes to the premise your scene partner puts in front of you and build on it. Think about your actions in terms of your relationship to the other person, and most importantly, be in the moment."

We paired off and started doing scenes. My first scene was with a young guy. We couldn't find our rhythm. Things were going badly when he made a quip about "Your mother is dying from cancer."

It's one of those things people do when they can't think of something to say; they pick something dramatic. He'd voiced my worst nightmare. I couldn't find words to respond.

We stopped the scene. I let it go, and we started over. Starting over was something I'd have to learn to do when my mom passed. Our failed scene was an excellent lesson. Each misstep in improv presented a learning opportunity. It was a chance to question my approach to the craft. How could I build on the premise that was on the table? What could I do to deepen my connection with my scene partner? What actions and reactions would make things more real and ultimately funnier?

My heart raced, but I looked forward to seeing what was going to happen in each session. One night, I was a sad Yugoslavian princess and the next an overbearing woman running into a high school acquaintance.

My mother got sicker as the course progressed. Our hugs grew longer, our words fewer. I went to class no matter how drained I felt. One night, I was in a scene with an established member of the troop. I was his stalker, and we were stuck on a riverboat. He talked about how I was following him. I went with it and declared my profound love. He returned my affection with some funny references to our shared history. I pointed out that the boat's captain could marry us. End of scene. It worked. I'd said yes and learned that I didn't have to be funny. I just had to be in the moment.

These were the same lessons I learned while sitting with my mother. I had no control over her fate, but could be with her, read to her, share stories, and look into her eyes. Meeting her where she was and loving her with everything I had was my mission. I could be present. I could be in the moment and just respond to what she offered, just like in improv class.

When we were together, I spent less time losing myself in the comfort of the Walton's on the television screen, and more time holding Mom's hand, bringing her favorite caramel donuts, and telling her how much I loved her.

We didn't get our miracle, but I found a deeper sense of faith. I can make the most of what is in front of me. I can say yes to life and to loss. I can be in the moment, no matter how hard it is. And because I am present, I can make new memories that sustain me in the face of loss.

***

Ellen Birkett Morris is the author of *Lost Girls: Short Stories*, stories about female strength and resilience, winner of the Pencraft Award and finalist for the Clara Johnson Award. Her fiction has appeared in *Shenandoah*, *Antioch Review*, *Notre Dame Review*, and *South Carolina Review*, among other journals. She is a winner of the Bevel Summers Prize for short fiction. Ellen received an Al Smith Fellowship from the Kentucky Arts Council.

Ellen is also the author of *Abide and Surrender*, poetry chapbooks. Her poetry has appeared in *The Clackamas Literary Review*, *Juked*, *Gastronomica*, and *Inscape*, among other journals. Morris won top prize in the 2008 Binnacle Ultra-Short Edition and was a finalist for the 2019 and 2020 Rita Dove Poetry Prize. Her poem "Abide" was featured on NPR's *A Way with Words*.

Her essays have appeared in AARP's *The Ethel*, *Oh Reader magazine*, and on National Public Radio. You can learn more about Ellen at her website https://ellenbirkettmorris.ink/ and on Instagram https://www.instagram.com/ellenbirkettmorris/

Ellen holds an MFA in creative writing from Queens University-Charlotte.

17 | Little Things by Mark Johnston

A mutual friend invited Carmen to a high-school graduation party we were hosting. I offered to pick them up and was smitten with Carmen at first sight. She exuded kindness, her smile was simultaneously bashful and filled with joy, and her laugh came easily, a sparkling, ascending cascade of sound that would carry her head backwards with mirth. I decided to impress her. Being eighteen and stupid, that meant driving as fast as possible and getting into a street race with my buddy, who tagged along in his car. We rounded the bend of Crowchild Trail at over 100 km/h. Suddenly, a wall of stalled traffic appeared in front of me, and I was forced to nearly ram the brake pedal through the floor of the vehicle. As everyone else in the car set about razzing me for my foolishness with a stream of creative expletives and jokes, Carmen looked at me and joined in. And thus, I fell in love. Though the reasons remain a mystery to me even to this day, Carmen fell in love with me, too, and we've been together ever since.

Over the next thirteen years of ups and downs, Carmen and I dreamt of having kids. During long drives to the mountains or her family's home in Edmonton, we envisioned our future family. We'd teach our two, maybe three kids about hiking and bear safety and camping. Their eyes would shine with that sort of wonder we all lose on the road to shitty adulthood. Vicariously, we would see the world anew.

***

The Sunrise Room lurks in the depths of the Foothills Hospital, a greedy and gaping hallway that ironically lacks any windows. I couldn't figure out how it got its name and pondered the question from an uncomfortable chair, gazing around the dim gloom of unadorned walls. Breathing in the sterile air, I decided it must be something to do with hope. I guess you need it when you sit there, waiting to speak to an oncologist about just how fucked you and your loved ones are. The Sun*set* Room has its own ironic implications.

"Why serenity sand?" I asked Carmen, breaking the oppressive quiet as I turned a booklet over and over in my hands, its cover adorned with wavey sand and little pebbles. Oddly, I almost wished we weren't alone, that there was somebody, anybody, else there with us. Yet to have company would mean nothing but more hearts about to break.

"I dunno," Carmen said. She glanced at the book in my hands and scowled slightly at the words emblazoned across the top: *Dealing with Cancer.*

"You know what would be better?"

"What?"

"A picture of Arnold Schwarzenegger looking all sad. Then the caption could read: Turns out… it *was* a tumah."

Carmen burst out laughing, and I smiled.

"And the doctors could wear trench coats," she added, "and call themselves *tumahnators.*"

"Carmen?" A nurse interrupted our laughter as she stepped into the hallway, chart in hands, a practiced smile set firmly in place. Carmen and I fell silent and applied porcelain masks of our own.

Carmen's voice quivered, "yes."

"Follow me, please." The nurse led us through a door into a room with a bed and chairs. The air was sour with antiseptic, and the lack of décor extended in from the hall. Everything looked dated and worn, sanded down by anguish and fear. VCT tile clacked under foot, patterned with flecks of muted color lost in a sea of filthy grey. I almost giggled at the thought that those tiles are likely chock full of asbestos, cancer on cancer in this strange place of bitter irony.

"The doctor will be in shortly," the nurse simpered. I almost told her I didn't want to see him. Bad news is just a rumor until given teeth. Inevitably, Dr. Boucharet stepped in, and the teeth gnashed.

"So, we can confirm that this is benign multicystic peritoneal mesothelioma," he began after introducing himself. "It's exceedingly rare. Mesothelioma is what most people know as the asbestos cancer, caused by breathing in fibers. The oddity of *your* condition is that it's not in the lungs." Carmen and I let out an audible breath. "It's in your peritoneum—the lining around your abdomen." His face softened suddenly. "It's also on your ovaries."

Honestly, I remember little after this point. I know only the gist of his awful words. I recall Carmen's hand tightening on mine, our white fingertips, and a dull ringing emanating from some deep, unseen tunnel. A med student in the room grabbed tissues from the bedside table and offered them to Carmen. My face reddened as I realized she was crying while I sat motionless. I slid my arm around her shoulders and squeezed. All I wanted to do was cry with her, but I didn't do that. *Men* don't do that, at least according to Hollywood. We are stoic in the face of cancer and the death of our future children.

My dad once lay in a bed like the one next to me in that room. He slipped into the abyss with multiple myeloma wrapped around his ankles, its teeth sunk deep into withering flesh. He didn't cry once.

I was nineteen when Grandma called me from her cancerous deathbed.

"Are you crying?" she asked as I blubbered into the receiver.

"Well, yeah!"

"Oh, stop it with that shit. This is nothing but a little thing, Mark. Nothin' but a little thing."

As Boucharet told us that Carmen would require a hysterectomy and we'd be referred to a fertility expert if we wanted, it didn't feel like a little thing. It felt like the sun was setting. Still, I couldn't cry.

Although we often describe time as currency to be spent or saved, it's much simpler than that; time is a one-way line filled with mockery. Carmen and I dreamt of children, but I procrastinated because I'm an author.

"We need a house first."

"Once I'm finished school."

Like my daydreams of becoming a famous author or revered musician or both, my children could remain alive and unstained in the realm of fantasy. If they became real, they could be harmed. Or worse, they might learn that their father is a bitter misanthropist. Worse still, they might become like me: fat, jaded and angry, yet somehow possessed with the audacity to walk like an emperor without his whisperer. Time is a tyrant with fear in its right hand. With a terrible blow, it had struck the heads of my phantom children.

When $20,000 didn't materialize in our accounts for in vitro or adoption, we found ourselves in yet another medical office. This room was brightly lit and carpeted, its walls a crisp, clean off-white. No beds or machines, just a desk and a doctor smiling behind it. Dr. Yen possessed one of those rare smiles, not made of clay or porcelain. She looked over our chart, her brow furrowed.

"What the actual hell is benign multicystic peritoneal mesothelioma!?" she asked. We laughed and explained.

"Damn," she replied when we'd finished.

"Yeah, we're not fans," Carmen said.

"Well, here's the thing. I'm seeing a critical keyword: benign. They've done scans, right?" We nodded. "It ain't growing. It's not spreading. Why does Boucharet want to go in guns blazing?"

The question honestly hadn't occurred to us. An oncological surgeon throws big, scary, cancerous words at you and says you need surgery. You don't question it. At least we didn't.

"Wait... are you saying we can wait?" I asked tentatively.

"I'm saying this guy's a surgeon looking at a once-in-a-lifetime cancer case; he's chomping at the bit to get in there and publish it."

"Asshole!" Carmen spat.

Yen softened her face and tone. "No, no, just ambitious like the rest of us. But look, if you want children, I don't see why you can't. Let's get you on hormone therapy and make it happen, yeah? Hell, with a little luck, you could have a baby within the year and then the cutter can dig in."

I've never known words to shine, but that room got brighter as she spoke. Maybe it was the sunrise. Carmen and I embraced, and for a moment, the corners of my eyes itched.

***

The ultrasound technician entered, flooding the darkened room with sudden light. She greeted us and gave some directions, hardly noticing how we held our breath. She didn't see white fingertips or feel the weight of impending tragedy. Carmen lay on the bed next to me and we interlaced our hands, hearts beating a disjointed paradiddle.

Weeks earlier, we'd succeeded in our very first round of hormone therapy. Of all my memories, few are clearer than when she interrupted my music writing and handed me the test. Her eyes were wide, unmoving. A smile twitched against flushed cheeks. I glanced down and saw that blessed +.

"That was so immediate!" I cried while launching to my feet and burying Carmen in a hug. I squeezed hard, then instantly relented, and touched her belly, whispering an apology to a speck of DNA not yet able to hear.

But two weeks later, the technician couldn't find the baby a bit of plastic had promised us. Another visit with Doc Yen; same room, new tone. It was still bright, but I smelled traces of that familiar sterile odor in the air. I noticed the carpet was discolored in a path leading to our chairs, and that the door was cleanest around its handle. Somewhere deep in the basement, a furnace rumbled and roared. Its breath through the grates sounded an awful lot like grinding teeth.

"The pregnancy..." Dr. Yen began quietly, without a smile. "May not be viable. We need to wait two weeks and try again. Don't lose hope."

And so we found ourselves in the same ultrasound room as before, two weeks later. Sterile. Dim. Stains hidden by the lack of light.

"There they are," the tech whispered. A little whitish-grey blob appeared on the screen, fuzzy and shifting, but there with a beating heart and a little yolk sac and a spine. Honest to God, it looked like a tiny little heart, but we spoiled the image in our excitement, knocking the tech's hand aside as we rushed to hug and kiss and weep. Tears exploded out of my eyes, unrestrained, unashamed. Together, Carmen and I sobbed joyfully.

"Mom and Dad," the tech said with a genuine smile, "meet baby. It's about the size of a blueberry."

Our little blueberry, awash in greyish blue and black, fuzzy like static, lit up the room. Suddenly, I didn't care if the sun was setting or rising or how much I cried. I didn't care that I was scared, because Carmen was there and we were a team, one always brave when the other couldn't find the capacity to be so. We could handle anything together, be it cancer or an overly ambitious hike, or a tiny human. I'd misunderstood Grandma J's final lesson, and I resolved to teach this heart-shaped cluster of cells just one thing: The sun rises and sets, there is cancer, there is death, there are hospital rooms and doctor's offices, there are fat misanthropists and emperors, there are mountains taller than them all, and there is time. These are very small indeed.

Tears are big.

***

Mark Johnston recently graduated from Mount Royal University in Calgary, Alberta, Canada. He obtained a bachelor's degree in history and creative writing. While attending MRU, he authored the short story, *The Thief, the Crier, and those Damned Dark Ages*, which won the Lynn Fraser Memorial Award for Humor through *FreeFall Magazine*.

When he isn't working at his new career as a historical researcher, Mark loves to write and play music, hike in the Rocky Mountains, and play board games with his friends.

For those wondering how the preceding story ends, Mark lives in Calgary with his partner, Carmen and their beautiful two-month-old son, Tristan Wayne Craig Johnston. They are excited to get Tristan out into the mountains for some fun, adventure, and, hopefully, some mischief.

18 | Finding Baby by Mary Christine Kane

My parents and I started an evening walk when we came across a small flash of yellow, bolting across the road. My mom cried out, "Whoa! Who's this little guy?" My dad jogged over to head a small duckling off with his feet and directed her back to the grass.

That might have been the end of our encounter, but the baby cuddled up against my dad's hairy, sandaled feet. We joked she was asking, "Are you my mommy?"

We wondered, where was her mom? Was the duckling cold? Did she need help? I struggled with leaving the duckling because we were on a thin strip of grass surrounded on three sides by busy roads. I feared she would get run over or fall into the sewer grate and get trapped. She was quite young, perhaps only a few days old.

I googled, "What do you do if you find an orphaned duckling?" Although the advice varied, one element was consistent: ducklings are always best off with their moms. We scoured behind bushes and tall grasses for any signs of a nest, our new friend waddling behind us. After a while, my dad cupped the duckling in his hands to warm her while she peeked her head out, chirping. We hoped her mom would recognize the sound.

The pretty June day turned to dusk. We weighed what to do next. My dad suggested we leave her. She would either make it or she wouldn't.

"That's how nature works," he said. "But I'm not sure you'll be able to do that."

I understood but I also thought, *I am part of nature too*. And I might be able to help our new friend. I needed to try.

My parents went home. I walked around looking for the duckling's mother until it was dark, and I was full of mosquito bites. The fuzzy yellow baby had drifted off to sleep in my cupped palms.

Sneaking past my two cats, I brought her inside. I punched holes in a shoebox and laid her on a blanket with a small stuffed dog to cuddle, which she immediately did.

I learned from online research that she could easily die during the night. She could choke while drinking from the shallow dish of water I gave her, since her mom had likely not yet taught her how to drink. She could die from cold given her body wasn't able to regulate heat. I was quite worried. This helpless little being depended on me. I reasoned, if the universe had chosen me to take care of her, the universe would help me.

As the duckling cuddled up to her new stuffed friend and slept, I called my friend Annette for advice. Annette had rescued many animals and knew some of the local resources. To my surprise, Annette's friend was raising ducks a few weeks older than my baby. Within an hour, I met her friend, Faye, in a Home Depot parking lot. The universe had sent someone to help us.

When I reached Faye's car, I saw a tall cardboard box with three duck heads sticking out of the top.

"This is the welcome committee," she said and smiled. "I hope they will make her feel comfortable."

Faye did not know if the older ducks would accept or reject the baby. We were hopeful. She and her twin teenage daughters took tender care of the duckling throughout the night, making sure their newcomer was comfortable and safe. The duckling nuzzled them and warmed herself under their heat lamp. Faye and her daughters knew how to give her water, leaning her head back so she would swallow without choking. In the morning, the baby duck heartily enjoyed her first hard-boiled egg.

The older ducks accepted the baby readily and took care of her, too. They put her in the middle of their ducky pile. Faye sent a picture.

"Your duckling is going to be just fine," she wrote. "We named her, Baby."

The next day I walked by the area where we found Baby to see if mother had appeared. I saw another duckling instead, the same size as ours, upside down in the sewer grate. My eyes welled up; it was so painful to see the beautiful, bright yellow darling lifeless against the ugly metal grate. It seemed proof the mother couldn't get back to her babies. I wondered if the siblings would have been better off if they had stayed together. I thought it more likely that neither would have made it more than a day or two. At least we had saved one.

Back at Faye's, within days, Baby learned to swim in Faye's Pond. Baby learned to fly. I got pictures and videos all summer, and it gave me great joy to hear she was doing so well. As she grew, Faye said Baby showed herself to be the bravest of the bunch. Also, the loudest! Even though she was the youngest, she was the first to jump into the pool, the first to swim underwater, and when beginning to fly, she fearlessly soared higher than the others. As her feathers grew in, Faye discovered Baby was female, which was what we guessed all along.

At the end of the season, when the lakes were freezing over, we waited to see if Baby would fly away like Faye's other ducks. Finally, one day, she did. We were happy because that's the natural order of things. Of course, we also worried, which was equally natural.

It turns out Baby was just fine because the next Spring she waddled up to Faye's door asking for peas. Baby hung around all summer, coming and going as she pleased, sometimes bringing friends. I was delighted we had given Baby another year.

And blessings of blessings, Baby came back a second year. She circled for weeks, waiting for the ice to break on Faye's Pond, quacking her hellos. This time she brought a friend who Faye and I affectionately referred to as "boyfriend," since they were always together.

Soon after, I got a text from Faye, "We're going to be duck grandmas!"

Baby made a nest in a nearby tree, and Faye and I nervously waited to see if Baby could protect her brood until they hatched. Several weeks later, one by one, seven ducklings made the twenty-foot jump. When each was on the ground, mother made her way to the pond with all seven ducklings waddling in a row behind her.

We didn't see Baby and her family for the rest of the summer. We were in a drought and the pond water was low. Faye guessed Baby found a better place to raise her ducklings. We hope she will come back and use the same nest next year, as they often do. We are still like nervous mothers, worried that she won't. We take comfort in knowing our small act has expanded to impact seven more lives.

Faye and I continue to text but now we talk about more than just ducks. Because we are friends. I share the latest challenges with my foster cats, and she updates me about her daughters. They are in college now and learning to fly themselves. That little fuzzy flash of yellow didn't just lead me to take care of her, she led me to a new friend.

I keep a picture of Baby on my office wall. She is about four days old, asleep in the grass. She is innocent and beautiful and perfect. It's a reminder to me of the power of the universe and that I never know in what beautiful ways it will conspire to help when I follow my heart.

***

Mary Christine Kane lives in Minneapolis, Minnesota where she works as a marketing consultant and volunteers for Pet Haven of Minnesota, an animal rescue organization. Through Pet Haven, Mary fosters cats and kittens and she mentors new volunteers.

Mary is a Moth winning storyteller and competed in the Minneapolis' 2022 Moth Grand Slam, held in the Guthrie Theater. Her essays and poetry have appeared in numerous anthologies and journals, including *Plainsong; Mutabilis Press; Bluestem*; *The Buffalo Anthology, Right Here, Right Now*; *Ponder Review* and others.

Between the stars where you are lost, Mary's poetry chapbook, was published by Finishing Line Press. She earned an MFA in writing from Hamline University in Saint Paul, Minnesota.

Mary can be found online at: MaryChristineKane.com.

19 | Hand Foot Hand by Deborah Kent

"Your parents are wonderful!" Neighbors used to say to me.

"They're just amazing," my Brownie leader exclaimed.

I even heard it from salespeople when we were out shopping.

One day late in the summer, the whole family went back-to-school shopping for all the kids. I was entering fourth grade, and my brother Zach was going into second. Gordy, the youngest, was starting kindergarten. We'd been slogging through all those old New Jersey stores like Haynes and Bamburgers, when we lurched into Tom McCann's for their fall sale. I was bored and whiny. Zach and Gordy were fighting. Mom snapped at us, and then Dad said, "Shape up, kids, or we're going straight home after this! No Dairy Queen!"

There I was, squeezing my hot, tired feet into one more pair of penny loafers, and the shoe store man said, "Your parents are wonderful!"

I thought, *what on earth are you talking about?*

Sometimes my parents were annoying, like many parents. Sometimes they were just plain mean, like when they said, "No, you can't get a hamster! Remember what happened when you got the one white mouse that turned out to be pregnant?" Sometimes they were okay, even sort of cool. But all the stuff people said about wonderful—it gave me a creepy feeling. I knew it had to do with me and Gordy. We weren't the children people dreamed of getting when kids were handed out. We were the kind of kids who ended up in special classes on the first floor over in Paterson.

On the first floor at our school, they sorted us into different groups of specialness. They had classes for kids who were deaf or who had cerebral palsy, they had a room for all those kids whom people today call developmentally delayed. And there was our class, for blind kids who learned braille and touch typing. We had our own special lunchroom and special playground.

Sometimes people whispered about me and Gordy and how our parents must have felt about us. They thought we couldn't understand. They would say things like, "It must have been such a shock!" "And they have no idea the cause . . ."

Parents weren't expected to rally after having one of us, let alone two! But there we were, just another back-to-school family at Tom McCann's.

People never told my brother Zach about his wonderful Mom and Dad. Zach, the middle kid, was the only one with functioning retinas. Every morning he walked to our neighborhood school in Little Falls, half a block down our street and a shortcut through the woods. Gordy and I had to wait for the special bus that took us to our special class.

Every June when school finished, our lives were transformed. My family spent a month each summer at Green Pond, a spring-fed glacial lake in the hills of Morris County. The summer I was ten, Mom managed the move; Dad would come up later, after work. The car was packed to the roof with suitcases, boxes, fishing poles, towels, blankets, and toys along with the dog and three kids. Somehow, we all managed to squeeze in among the luggage.

As we climbed Green Pond Road, the air grew cooler, and the scent of the woods floated through the open car windows. My ears popped as the car climbed higher.

"We're going through Tree Tunnel!" Zach cried at the famous spot where arching branches met above the road.

Before long, we scrambled out of the car.

"Nobody goes in empty-handed!" Mom said.

Once we dropped our bundles in the kitchen we pleaded, "Can we go swimming? Please?"

"Not now!" Mom said. "Go find something to do. Let me sort things out around here."

Zach and I wandered outside to find something to do. "Let's climb up to the Blue Flag!" Zach said.

Along the West Shore of Green Pond, the Great Glacier deposited vast boulders ten thousand years ago, creating an enormous rock wall. Generations of teenagers climbed these rocks with cans of paint to leave messages for posterity. People read them aloud as we passed below in the canoe: "Betty loves Joe," "Peppertown," "Go Hornets!" Nobody knew when someone painted a Blue Flag up at the top of this rocky crag.

I poked my head in the back door. "We're going up to the Blue Flag, okay?" I called.

"Okay." Mom's muffled reply came from behind the pantry door.

"Me, too!" Gordy yelled. We pretended we didn't hear him. I grabbed Zach's hand, and we made a dash for the West Shore path.

Water lapped close on our left, and on our right the rocks loomed, casting an echo with every footstep. At last Zach said, "We can go up this way. There's a big rock in front of your right foot. Stand on there and pull yourself onto the ledge by your shoulder."

We climbed slowly and carefully, Zach giving me directions all the way. Hand . . . foot . . . hand . . . foot . . .. The world dwindled down to Zach's clear instructions, "Reach up with your right hand . . . over wide with your left foot . . . down a little more, there, that's it . . ."

At one point Zach got stuck, and I reached down so he could hang onto my hand and haul himself up. It helped that I was taller than he was, with longer legs and arms.

We paused on a ledge to catch our breath and Zach said, "Copperheads live up here."

He was right. Almost every summer somebody at Green Pond got bitten.

"Do you see any?" I asked.

"I don't think so," he said. "But they kind of blend in."

I took the next handhold gingerly, braced for a cold, scaly slither and the sting of fangs. But my hand found rock, safe and solid. "Go away, snakes!" I shouted, and we kept climbing.

At last, we crawled on our stomachs over one final, rounded boulder. We found ourselves on a high, flat rock, warmed by the sun. The wind swept around us.

"We're really high up!" I marveled.

"Right under the sky," Zach said.

"Where's the Blue Flag?" I asked.

It was painted on the side of the rock next to us. I crouched down and followed Zach's hand, but my fingers couldn't make out the shape of the image. I didn't mind. We had reached it. That was what mattered.

That day, I discovered that getting down is a lot more difficult than climbing up. At one point, I hung onto a rock while my legs flailed in the air. I couldn't pull myself back up or find a way down. I was terrified I'd fall into a vast field of bone-snapping, skull-cracking rocks.

But Zach reassured me. "Just let go," he said. "It's only four inches."

My fingers couldn't hang on any longer. I gave up my hold and found myself upright and safe on a wide, friendly ledge. I rested until my heart stopped pounding. Not far below now, water lapped gently.

We continued our downward climb. Foot . . . hand . . . foot . . . hand . . .

Finally, I stood on solid ground, the familiar West Shore path. The rock wall loomed above us, the lake rippled a welcome, and we scampered back to the cottage.

Mom was sweeping the front porch. "Where have you two been?" she demanded.

"We did it!" we yelled. "We climbed all the way!"

"All the way where?"

"To the Blue Flag!"

"You did *what*?" Mom exclaimed.

"You said it was okay," I reminded her.

"I *never* said that!" Mom insisted. "I must have misheard you. It was *not* okay! It was dangerous! Don't you have better sense? Are you alright?"

We were fine. We were exhilarated! We had climbed up to the Blue Flag, just like the teenagers did! And we had done it all by ourselves.

When Dad arrived that night, we told him all about it. We went out on the dock so he could look up at where we'd been, and he gave a long whistle. "Wow!" he said proudly. "That was some climb. That was *some* climb, alright."

"It's not fair!" Gordy complained. "I never get to have any fun!"

That week the weather was beautiful. We swam laps between the docks, built a giant sandcastle on the beach, and played a Monopoly marathon. And life was going to get even better; The Conovers were going to visit that weekend.

The Conovers were old friends of Mom and Dad, and their three children were similar in age to us. We'd have a new set of kids to play with. Dad pitched a tent in the back yard so the six of us could camp out, leaving the boring old cottage to the grownups. Mom arranged to borrow Grandpa's motorboat so we could take everyone water-skiing on Friday afternoon. But how would we entertain them on Saturday?

"A cook-out maybe?" Mom suggested.

Gordy said, "We can take them to the Blue Flag." He wasn't a kid who forgot things.

How about we go out fishing?" Dad offered.

"They'd like to go to the Blue Flag!" Gordy said.

"We could . . ." Mom began.

"We all could . . ." Dad started to say.

107

"Blue Flag! Blue Flag!" Gordy chanted. "We're going to the Blue Flag!"

Zach and I picked up the chant. "Blue Flag! Blue Flag! Blue Flag!"

"What do you think?" Dad asked Mom.

"I haven't been up there since I was sixteen . . ." she replied.

We waited as they telegraphed back and forth.

"Maybe . . ." Dad said.

"Something different," said Mom.

Finally Dad said, "Oh, why not?"

On Saturday morning, our noisy, laughing cavalcade trooped along the West Shore path—four adults and six kids, two of whom were blind. I realized that my parents really *were* wonderful.

When Mom and Dad began their long life together, they didn't know they shared a rare recessive gene that would affect two of their future children. But perhaps they understood that they shared something else, a spirit of adventure. They weren't afraid to embrace the unexpected. When life greeted them with surprises, they rose to the challenge. Where some would have cried, they discovered laughter and a path through the tangles.

So we all headed up the rocks to the Blue Flag that Saturday morning. Hand . . . foot . . . hand . . . foot . . . hand . . .

***

Deborah Kent began her professional career as a social worker at University Settlement House on New York's Lower East Side. Later she moved to San Miguel de Allende in Mexico and devoted herself to writing. She is the author of nearly two dozen young-adult novels and numerous nonfiction titles for middle-grade readers. Over the past several years, she has branched into writing personal essays and pieces for live performance. Her work has appeared in The McGuffin, Adelaide Review, Persimmon Tree, Damselfly, and in several anthologies. She lives in Chicago with her husband, children's author R. Conrad (Dick) Stein.

20 | Letting Go by L.B. Johnson

It was a blue shirt–old, weathered, but not worn or laundered since it first took up residence in my closet. Worn on a fall evening long ago.

Overhead, a sound passes by, a gnashing crunch of tires meeting gravel, the sound dying away, not to return. From somewhere close, a deep sigh, my own, or perhaps the wind in the trees—shivering stalks against the sky. The day the shirt took up residence, tears came. But tears will eventually slow to a quiet seeping of dreams against a pillow in the night; a muffled resignation that you hope no one sees traces of in the day. Those are the days that grow round and monotonous when life slows to one of quiet acceptance.

When someone leaves, you go through the motions of life. You endure your days, fueled by habit, filling up the hours until you can fall asleep at night and not dream of the warm body that hasn't lain next to you for so long. It rarely works. Those are the nights when the loneliness sticks to your skin like a burr, when all you want is to shout to the heavens or speak to that person who became part of you, then left, taking with them small bits of flesh, exposing nerve endings to the cold night air. But you don't. Life goes on, and you listen again for that crunch of gravel that is only the delivery man, as the vines creep against the house, growing wild, overflowing to your heart and constricting it.

But there are chores to do. They do not wait. The smell of oak, smoked fire already burning as I try to penetrate the honeyed wood, its core as hard as iron, the axe aimed down, straight to the heart of the knot. The axe bites and the wood falls to pieces, and the things you cannot ignore burn into you.

Finally, after a dark and introspective night, you wake to the sound of warm rain beating against the eaves, your body flush with dreams in a tangle of sheets. Not remembering the details of that night's dream, but just the feeling it imprinted on you, as you breathe in wakefulness, bringing back memories long forgotten. Dreams of longing, of desire, fleeting things, reflections in a river, seen for just a second, then swept away in the solitary stream that was your day. For it seems you can hardly remember what it was like when you felt that way, when a simple smell touched the place where that feeling was, when a touch was slight and quick as fabric against your skin, as soft and fleeting as a bird's wings against your face. You quicken to the memory. And hope takes wing.

I find the shirt while cleaning out to prepare for a yard sale. In the suddenness of its discovery, it trickles through my hands like tears, puddling on the ground as the memory awakes.

That evening so long ago was much like other autumn evenings, with the air crisp and cold, brushed with the scent of kindling alight. You too have had an evening like that, where anticipation waits like an embrace, ticklish like a stray hair brushing against the back of your neck. An evening where you were swept away for only a moment, which has repeated itself, minute by minute in your memory, wrong place, wrong moment. One of those times you wish you could turn time back on itself, as if you had never been there at all.

I'd heard he was in town on business. How long had it been since I'd made that decision to end things? I was wrapped up in my career, and when the whole commitment thing loomed on the horizon, I had to decide. So I made the call that was one of the hardest I had ever made. I said I couldn't see him anymore. He sounded hurt and also relieved. He sounded unbearably tired. But mostly relieved. I wasn't ready for anything serious, not like he wanted. After all the changes in my life, a new career, and aging parents, I wasn't ready to give him what he wanted. Yet. So I cut the tether and let him go.

Renovating an old house became my sanctuary, the power of saw and sweat the tithing of my soul. My mind was desperate to sort out the past before I decided about the future, one that could change not just my life, but another person's. Sometimes, creating something with hard work and wood helped. I tried not to think of the last months since we said goodbye on the phone. It was a conversation that made me want to crawl into my car and drive until the horizon filled my entire world. Why is escape so difficult? Finding peace? Why can I sometimes only find that in the power of a hammer, the scent of black powder, the feel of a steering wheel under my hand? Forces that, for an instant, I can control. But I knew I did the right thing, for to promise something to someone who cared so deeply, when I was not ready to give it, was the cruelest of good intentions.

So I went back to the life of fire and wood. As I swung the axe into another small log, I thought of his last words "I will come back, you know." The words were like a hand against my back, a feeling lingering across my shoulders, down my arms that whispered their aching promise. But months passed, and when I realized I was finally ready for what he was asking, the phone lay silent.

I was finishing the second coat of paint when the phone finally rang. "I'm in the neighborhood. Can I see you? There's something I need to tell you." He sounded wistful, happy, and my heart unexpectedly missed two cylinders as I suddenly and truly smiled for the first time in months. I placed the piece of drying work aside, racing around trying to compose my thoughts, my regrets, and the decision I should have made when it was offered. I needed to prepare a house in just a few minutes and make some supper. How long had it been since I'd had someone over? Soon the kitchen would be warm with spice; the ripe juice of something succulent bursting on my lips.

111

Before I showered and changed, he was waiting on my doorstep. That blue shirt. The way he stood, his inviting smile and eyes the color of an evening sky, his body relaxed in a pair of khakis. He was smiling a boyish, hesitant grin. The sight of him eases the memory of tears and turns my empty heart into longing. Was that you I said goodbye to?

I pull back; this situation is not covered in those etiquette books my grandmother relied on. I look into his smile, struggling to see his motives, searching his eyes to define my own. For there is so much unsaid there, so many questions, his questions, mine. My fear? His? These are the intangible walls that distance us, the walls of heartache made of concrete laced with steel; impenetrable.

Let me just touch you, I say silently. Tear down that wall; rip the concrete from its foundation. Words only heard in my soul. But as if reading my thoughts, he pulls me towards him in the familiar hug of a friend. I hear my heart pounding as he opens his arms to envelop me. He finds a dab of thick yellow paint tattooed on my cheek, just underneath my eye. A kiss lands nearby. My lips silently call to him, as his proximity encourages me to reveal my feelings. But I don't. I have to stay in control, I tell myself.

I draw him inside, into a house that now feels like home.

"I just wanted to see you in person," he says. "I wanted to hear your voice."

I can't keep the words inside much longer. *I was an idiot. I love you. I'm ready.* I want to just get it out. But I keep quiet, afraid to interrupt.

"I wanted to be the one to tell you in person," he says as he takes off his outer blue shirt, with the precision of movement and form that made me feel both safe and shy. Setting it on the chair, he stands before me, looking happy and hopeful in his work-worn pants and T-shirt. The words hang in the air, dense with longing, waiting to be breathed in deeply.

When you're young, no one tells you that the true story of love does not involve a fairytale ending like at the movies. You had rehearsed your love story over and over in your head, speaking the words you scripted so carefully, waiting for what you know he will say back. Then, braced with the chill fall air, I open my mouth to speak, to finally say the words. He speaks first. The words are not what I expected.

"I'm getting married."

My eyes follow his voice as it drifts out the window and fades. All I can see are dying leaves, windswept trees, barren fields, and desolate plans. I step away from the warmth of the room so he doesn't see my shock, and I face the yard, as a tree outside explodes into flight when hundreds of birds are startled into escape. There I stand, that spot of paint on my face, a dam holding back the tears, as I stare at a tree now empty of life but for one lone bird. I turn back to him.

"Are you okay? You look pale. I knew you'd be happy for me."

The words bit my skin like insects, drawing blood from veins with little to spare. I couldn't wait to get the door closed behind him. Attempting a smile, I told him I had to go. Something had come up, but congratulations, honestly. I didn't cry until the sound of tires on gravel was only a memory.

I looked back at the chair and realized he left his shirt. It is a shirt with the clear blue color of tears, one left in the wake of his words of goodbye.

Now, on another chill evening, the house silent as always, I hold the blue fabric of that shirt close to me, breathing in the heat we might have made and the smell that still clings to it. Hanging in my closet, it is a remembrance of scent and touch. The cloth is faded and fragile, like all dreams. Then, finally, I put it away, deep in a drawer, and find that over time its touch only creates a dim memory on my fingers.

I get up from my chair and open the curtains. I look at a sun I have not seen in two days, as winter's last wind hollowed the remaining light out of the sky. In the distance, the sound of a church bell, a deliberate note blowing free, like snow from a winter branch. Somewhere within, a priest lifts the chalice—a shimmering gleam like warm rain that falls from the sky, as words of forgiveness are spoken and what's broken is healed.

I look out into the skies as the birds return to the tree.

***

L.B. "Brigid" Johnson is the best-selling author of both fiction and non-fiction including the Amazon #1 Best Seller, *The Book of Barkley– Love and Life Through the Eyes of a Labrador Retriever*, and her latest book, the international #1 Best Seller, *True Course: Lessons from a Life Aloft*. A two-time winner of the Reader's Favorite International Book Award and recipient of the 2020 Independent Author Network Gold Award for Outstanding Non-Fiction Young Adult, Ms. Johnson did not begin writing until her 40s. She left behind eighteen years as an airline captain to finish a doctorate in a Forensic Science field that does not involve a career in multiple time-zone changes and suspicious airport food. She lives in Chicago with her engineer husband. Restoring a 100-year-old Mission Bungalow keeps the creativity flowing and an assortment of rescue dogs ensures that her home may eventually be "done" but will never be "dog hair-free." Johnson donates 100% of the proceeds from her writing to animal rescue non-profits and Search Dog Foundation.

21 | A Love That's Grey–Blue by Kate MacLauchlan

The love of my grandmother, or Grammy, set the standard for all the loves that would come after, platonic or otherwise. Her love fit like the perfect fall coat: not smothering, not lacking, and highlighting the best parts of me.

I grew up in a landscape full of cows, cheerleaders, and football players. People migrate to Texas for the infinite blue skies, but a land so massive suffocated me in its vastness. I didn't take a liking to horseback riding, or 4H, like my peers. As a lover of stories, songs, and dancing, I felt like a weirdo. I convinced myself that some alien spaceship dropped me into a time and place that didn't suit me. However, I had one ally, one co-conspirator: my Grammy.

A New Jersey native, Grammy didn't blend easily into rural Texas either. Before I was born and after her husband passed away, she moved in with my family. She had a gorgeous set of grey-blue eyes, she was petite, and she had a potty-mouth. In fact, one of my favorite things I heard her say was, "That Robert Redford sure gives me a slick spot in the crotch!" She flirted shamelessly with the UPS delivery guy. She often forgot to take one curler (or two) out of her hair, and she always said the obvious. My family members rarely disclosed their feelings, but Grammy missed that memo. Her brusque delivery always caught them off guard. She was my hero.

As often as possible, I feigned some sort of illness, so that I could play hooky from school and hang out with Grammy. We waited for the coast to be clear, then we put away the Saltines and the Gatorade. She would make me a grilled-cheese sandwich because she always knew what I *really* wanted. We spent the day watching old movies like *Singin' in the Rain*, *An American in Paris*, *My Fair Lady*, and we debated over who we loved more. Was it

Gene Kelly? Donald O'Connor? Or Debbie Reynolds? The answer always changed, but one thing was certain: In those old movies, I found my people.

When I applied to colleges, I knew deep down where I wanted to go, but my parents wanted me nearby. My family is small and scattered sparsely across the country. How could I leave the little unit that was my mom, dad, big sister, little sister... and Grammy? It was a tender topic with my parents, but I couldn't shake the feeling that I belonged elsewhere. I applied secretly to a college just outside of New York City. They accepted me and planned to cover most of my tuition, except for a small portion. Thrilled and terrified, I pondered how to tell the news to my family.

That day came when, one day, my mom, sisters, Grammy, and I went to Bucca di Beppo. Over a big plate of chicken parmesan, I swallowed the lump in my throat and announced, "I'm going to New York! My mind's made up!"

The table fell silent. My sisters' silverware scratched their plates as they tried to twirl their spaghetti. Grammy sat smiling at me. My mother got up and excused herself to go to the restroom, which was code for, "I'm going to go cry now." My cheeks burned. I felt selfish. Then, Mom came back to the table and peppered me with questions.

"Have you visited the campus?" She asked.

"Nope!" I exclaimed.

"Have you given them a decision?"

"Yup!"

"How are you paying for the piece that's not covered by financial aid?"

"I'll get a job on or off campus—"

Grammy interrupted and held up her hand.

"I'm going to pay for it," she said decisively, looking at me knowingly with those grey-blue eyes.

"...because I want you to do it." she said.

Ever since that moment, I've searched for a love like that, a love that's just that easy. I wanted a fellow weirdo to *breathe* with, to eat a grilled cheese with, someone who understood what I *really wanted.*

I flew back and forth from Austin to New York. The first time I came home with a nose piercing, Grammy pretended to cry, but laughed. "Oh my God, Kaitlin, what have you done?" Then she chuckled and gave it a little tug. Other times I came home, wondering if it was a mistake for me to leave. She let me have my moment, hugged me, and then she patted my butt, because that's what grandmothers do. She gathered herself and said, "Ok now. Cut the bullshit...Chin up, kid." Another time, I came home for Spring Break. I touched down in Austin and gave Grammy a hug and a kiss. For a time, she'd been unwell, and that evening she decided to leave this world. I'd like to think she waited for me... and maybe for herself too, because she knew how devastated I would be if I couldn't say goodbye.

Years later, I had just finished an improv show. It was cold and rainy, and I was crabby. I didn't know what I was doing in New York anymore. I hopped on a Long Island Railroad train to Queens and headed home. Unbeknownst to me, the train was not going to stop at my station. I would have to get out at the next stop and return in the other direction.

Of course, I thought to myself. *Isn't that just fuckin great?*

I headed to the nearest door of the train car and the ticket collector came by and asked where I was heading. I kept my head down and grumbled, "Kew Gardens."

As I stared at my reflection in the train car door, to my surprise, the conductor stopped a train full of people so I could get off at my station. The ticket collector came to the door where I stood to unlock it.

"Have a good night," he said as the door opened.

I looked up and started to say, thank you, but my breath caught. I froze. This man had my grandmother's grey-blue eyes. I had never met him before, but there was no mistaking it. The eyes I was looking at were hers. I got off the train, and I sat on a bench for a long time, catching my breath.

I still have days where I get crabby and wonder what I'm doing. I still get frustrated, but I manage. And even though I don't really believe in the supernatural, I hang onto the hope that I'll get an unexpected push from a stranger with a familiar set of grey-blue eyes.

***

Kate MacLauchlan is currently working on her Master of Fine Arts in Creative Writing at Manhattanville College, where she received her B.A. in Dance and Theatre and B.A. in Spanish literature.

She wrote and performed sketch comedy and improv at The People's Improv Theater, Upright Citizen's Brigade, and Under St. Marks Theater in New York. She also danced and performed with Donofrio Dance Company.

She is an enthusiastic Moth member and storyteller and recently performed at the Magnet Theater.

In her day job, she is a television producer. She also spends a large portion of her time reading, playing bocce, and catering to her two Cavalier King Charles Spaniels, Penny and Theodore.

22 | Airborne by Dian Parker

I never saw this love coming, nor did I want it. I was an independent woman; successful, alone, and free. A life I had chosen. One day I was hanging around with my cat, living in a yurt on my land surrounded by cottonwoods and cedars, head gardener for three estates. The next moment I was living in a house with a different cat, in an aspen forest, lying in a man's arms, barely able to think. I no longer have my yurt, my land, or my cat. She died and I died. Transformed.

In the first year of our love, it was an effort to get things done and to make plans. My brain was floating in a diaphanous sea, bobbing up and down to the tides of his touch and gaze. When I finally got out of bed in the morning, I intended to vacuum the house and weed his garden. But when I looked at the floor and all those weeds, they seemed unimportant compared to walking in the field holding his hand. So I threw myself into the experience, losing myself. I gave up and surrendered to the moment.

He looked at me and I disappeared.

Love. Love. I did not know. I hadn't lived in a world where it existed. Warm feelings, yes, compassion, concern, tenderness. Longing to embrace a child or a tree, to stroke a wet cheek or a bruised knee. Laughter shared and gratitude expressed, long moments in meditation seeking, a heartfelt embrace. These and other spurts, came and went. But this! No gaps, no bare spaces, everything filled in, flowing, overflowing, spilling into everything. The rose on the windowsill became an altar. Our night ski through the silent snow became a religion in my brain. Baking bread offered a solution to the unified field theory. Cleaning the shower I would be so overcome with feeling, I'd have to sit down in the tub to catch my breath.

For the first year we continued this way. Rapt. Somehow, we managed to keep working.

One day, at the beginning of our second year together, we watched a documentary about Andy Goldsworthy, the sculptor who creates momentary works in nature. We decided to go on a short hike near Mount Rainier to create our own nature art. We figured a couple of hours, and return home before dark. That morning I'd made spanakopita, ready to pop in the oven when we got home.

The waterfall was only a thirty-minute drive from the house. While he drove, we talked about choice. "It's all a slip of the die, really," I said. "You make a particular choice and your whole world shifts. Most of the time we don't realize how radical our choices are."

"Yeah, I could slip and crash through a glass door and my whole life would change," he said.

We laughed and I kissed his neck.

After parking along the side of the road, we scrambled down a short hill to an old railroad bridge. The rushing winter river roared below as we walked along the ties. Climbing down snow-covered rocks, we came to the top of a thundering waterfall. We had to shout to be heard. Inspired by Goldsworthy, we built sculptures with twigs and fern fronds, spiraling them over shards of ice. We piled the botanical ice into towers. Tommy stood up to take pictures with his new camera.

A few moments later, I heard a strange sound. It was low and soft. Distant, faint, traveling away. It was a tiny sound above the roar of the falls. For years afterwards, I heard that sound in my head. The death moan.

My first thought was that he had fallen. No, that was impossible. I looked over my shoulder and he wasn't there. I crawled to the edge of the cliff and looked down. Yes. No. Yes. Under the water. In the pool at the base of the raging waterfall. I could just make out the hood of his purple sweatshirt bobbing on top of the turbulent water.

I crouched at the top of the cliff trying to comprehend.

In the next *instant,* I was sprawled across rocks at the base of the falls, pulling him out of the water. How did he get here? How did I?

My first thought was to hold him close, to warm his wet, icy body with my hot, panicked love. But I could see he was not all in one piece. He couldn't stand and his left arm was dangling at a weird angle. To further complicate my terror, we had no phone.

A hiker appeared. Where did he come from? He wrapped Tommy in a jacket and called 911. My love insisted he was ok and that the hiker should go. The hiker left and I poured my being into Tommy. After what seemed like several hours, I saw men on top of the cliff. A lot of men, all in uniform: EMTs, firemen, a forest ranger.

I waved frantically. The nine-man rescue team climbed down the high, steep, icy cliff, slowly, laboriously, with all their gear; large backpacks and a very long stretcher, which was good because Tommy is six-four. They worked quickly, stripping off his wet clothes. It was then I saw his left elbow protruding through the skin. Even though he couldn't move without intense pain, he refused painkillers. They strapped him down to the stretcher and put a brace around his neck.

Because the cliff was too steep and icy for the crew to climb carrying the stretcher with a body, the forest ranger bushwhacked a trail through the forest with a machete. It seemed to take several more hours to make our way through the dense trees and steep embankment where an ambulance waited in the middle of a cornfield. I had no idea where we were.

Adding to my already fractured state, they didn't let me go with him in the ambulance. One of the firemen hiked with me back to the road where our car was parked. Everything was ice, including my limbs, which weren't holding me up well. I'd also been hauling

Tommy's wet heavy clothes and one shoe in a black plastic bag for hours. He'd lost the other shoe in the water.

It was now dark. I got lost three times trying to find the hospital. It turned out he was not at the hospital that the ambulance driver told me. It was another hospital, half an hour away. I got lost twice again. When I finally got there, I learned he was in the trauma unit. Trauma? They wouldn't let me see him because we weren't married and who the heck was I anyway? I tried not to get hysterical. I begged and pleaded. For all I knew, he might be dead.

Finally they let me see him. A surgeon in a starched white shirt and tie stood over Tommy holding a bloody piece of white cloth. The incongruity made me want to faint but I still held on. The doctor proceeded to slowly tell me that Tommy broke his left ankle, six ribs, and shattered the bones in the left arm. The surgeon wanted to know if he should insert a titanium rod to hold Tommy's arm together. I asked Tommy. He said to call his sister, who's an EMT. I still didn't have a phone and the hospital wouldn't let me call long distance. I ended up telling the surgeon to do whatever he thought best.

Five hours of surgery later, the rod was inserted, the ankle set and bound in a cast.

For one month, Tommy lay flat on his back. He couldn't move his left arm and his hand was numb. It took six weeks for the ribs to heal so that he wasn't in excruciating pain every time he moved. I rented a wheelchair and pushed him around. After another month he was able to walk with a cane. This was when he insisted on going back to the falls. I did not want to go. I didn't ever want to go to that place again, but I wasn't about to let him go alone.

As we walked across the railroad bridge, he told me about his near-death experience underwater. He said that despite going through the six hours of rescue, the operation, months in bed, all the pain, the wheelchair and canes, his strongest memory was when he became conscious underwater.

He explained, "There were bubbles swirling in the darkness like stars in the sky. I didn't know what or where I was, I just knew I was experiencing something extraordinary. I was drawn towards a dark horizon. All I had to do was relax into it and every care and concern would be over. It was warm and inviting. But just as I began to allow myself to go in that direction, I felt a strong physical need for something. I didn't know what it was. I had a desperate urge in my chest and remembered that I needed to breathe. At that moment, all thoughts of that peaceful place vanished as I struggled to the surface and took in the first gasping breath of air. I saw you leaning over the edge of the pool and remembered who I was. I wanted to live."

At the end of the old railroad bridge, we hiked down the steep path. The river was racing wildly because of the recent heavy rain and snowmelt. We crawled to the edge of the cliff where the roaring water threw itself over. Where he had disappeared.

On our stomachs, we peered over the edge of the waterfall. Far below was the pool of water he fell into. It was a small round pool far below an extremely high cliff. We looked at one another in astonishment.

Tommy began climbing down. My legs shook. I felt traumatized and froze. He held me tight. Helping me climb down, I had to stop often, catching my breath. Finally, after an excruciating long climb down the cliff, we stood at the base of the falls. A furious mist from the thundering falls soaked our clothes.

We looked up.

This man next to me should be dead or at least paralyzed for the rest of his life. Instead, he was standing next to me, strong and upright. He had careened downward, bouncing off sharp slabs of rock that jutted out all the way down the cliff, ending in a small pool of icy water. We measured the drop with a rope–forty-five feet!

We've been together now nearly twenty years. We live 3,000 miles away from that waterfall. I joke now that his falling off the waterfall so early in our relationship was a test, and we laugh.

Maybe love saved his life. And taught me how to fly.

***

Dian Parker's essays and short stories have been published in *3:AM Magazine, The Rupture, Anomaly, Epiphany, Tiny Molecules, Burningword Literary, Brevity, Westerly, Critical Read, After the Art*, among others, and nominated for several Pushcart Prizes and Best of the Net. Her art writing and color essays are with Art & Object, Fine Books & Collections, Art New England, and others. Parker was gallery director at White River Gallery in Vermont, curating twenty exhibits. A fellow at the Vermont Studio Center, and an oil painter, she has had solo exhibits of her paintings in Vermont.

Parker has traveled extensively, sleeping in shepherd huts in Sinai and in the Valley of the Dead in Palmyra, Syria before ISIS bombed the ancient city, and she lived in the caves of Petra with Bedouins before they were forced into housing developments. Her travels have also taken her to Morocco, Mexico, Greece, Turkey, throughout Europe and the U.S.

She trained at the Royal Academy of Dramatic Art in London, and now studies with her mentor, writer Baron Wormser. Currently she lives in the hills of Vermont surrounded by forests, wildlife, and bird song. Visit her website: www.dianparker.com.

23 | Present by Darlene Williams

My mother slips away from my life when I am thirty-three—one week after Jeff and I get married. No, she is not at our wedding as we planned—her absence a hole in the day. No one speaks of it; everyone treads gently. We go to the hospital after the reception, play her the wedding recording, and give her gardenias—her favorite. The night she passes, Jeff drives us home from the hospital on the Northwest side of Chicago down to the far South suburbs. My eyes smudged, my shuddering continues as we pass the 95th Street exit and beyond. Saying nothing, he keeps his hand on my leg as the light rain, red taillights, and green road signs fly past us. My newlywed husband doesn't think I see his stealthy glances, his eyes wide at seeing how long I keep crying. I cannot talk. I have nothing to say. I am in front of an iron-clad black door that's sealed shut. When I can't breathe anymore, my nose fills. I stab at the glovebox, its mouth judders down, and I grab some Starbucks napkins. I clear my airways and slam the lock closed again. Every few minutes I stop, blow, take some clear breaths, and start again. Glovebox, napkins, blow, close. I look up as we turn onto our street. We pull into our one stall garage and a sigh escapes. My eyes are sore and tender to the touch. I am weary, and in my body, I feel an aching hole.

In the spring, I am laid off from my teaching job, which doesn't seem to matter much. The replacement job I get is not the one I want, but one the universe wants for me. I teach art part time to seventh graders in an affluent suburb. Home by 12:30, I spend my fall and winter afternoons raking through any tokens of memory my mother may have left for me. I look for notes, letters with her handwriting, or replay conversations. I try to manage this reflex to rummage through things, but never do. I want to latch onto pieces of her from things she owned, music, books, and movies she liked. I call her friends, my deep need preventing me from asking outright, but they eventually get around to her. They drop memory crumbs I eagerly pick up. I listen to a repetition of once annoying stories I've heard a million times, but now don't mind hearing.

Jeff, a solid presence, fills the chasm in my body that my mother leaves. I curl against his bulwark shoulder, and I meld into his strength and support. He becomes a repository, a vessel for all the weak and sad feelings I cannot contain. He accepts them, holds them, and then transfers my grief into something new and good.

I call my dad every night. As a newlywed, I grasp what he must be feeling. What would I feel like to have my husband taken from me? But my dad and I never talk about her or say her name. He doesn't bring her up, and I can't.

Now many years have gone by, and I know this is the worst time in grief—when you can't even look at a beloved's photograph or say their name.

Most weekends, Jeff and I drive the fifty miles to be with my dad and do things together, to get him back to engaging in life. We drag him to flea markets, watch movies together or go out to eat. The constant contact guides us both back to engaging with life. We have never been close, and we are building something new and strong. We move forward without her.

Two years pass. Jeff, my dad, and I attend my cousin Jason's wedding. My dad is seated with his sister while Jeff and I are at the cousin's table farther away. The other cousins have dispersed to different tables or gathered around the low-ceilinged room. The empty plates that held the chicken, potatoes, and pasta have been cleared, and we occupy that awkward time after they have cut the wedding cake and before the dancing. Jeff asks me if I want another drink; they have just reopened the bar.

"No," I answer. "The first two are enough." He stands putting both hands on the back of his chair, stops and looks down at me.

"Agnes," he says.

I am jolted when hearing my mother's name, the first time in months.

He continues, "I never met anyone like her, someone who could drink me under the table like your mom. Nobody has ever done that."

"Yes, you've said that before," I smile, looking down at the brown carpet and then at him. "What made you say her name?"

"Not sure," he says. His amber eyes hold my gaze while he loosens his tie from his collar. He is silent for a few beats, breathes out and says, "I never told you this."

I look up. "Told me what?"

"Remember that night we were in Scotland, you, your mom, and me? It was one of the last few days of our trip."

"Yeah, I remember."

"Remember the night you went upstairs right after dinner because you were tired, and your mom and I stayed in the bar?

So, we order drinks. Your mom has her usual small-airline bottles stashed in her purse. She orders a Southern Comfort, drinks half of it, and then reaches down to get one of her bottles and adds all the booze to her drink."

"She never traveled without them," I say with a laugh back in my throat.

"That night, she used up three or four airline bottles before we left. She dropped one, and the glass bounced and made a loud noise. Everyone turned around to look at us. I thought they were going to throw us out." He looks up with a low snicker. "We were in that hotel bar for almost three hours, and she didn't seem wasted, but I sure was." Jeff shifts his weight to his left leg.

"About two drinks in, we're talking about our trip, and she thanks me for driving so well on the left side of the road and for schlepping the luggage. Then, Agnes blindsides me. She leans in narrowing her eyes at me and says, 'Are you going to marry my daughter or *what*? I've been with you for the last two weeks. You both seem happy. Do you love her?'"

He glances at me and continues, "I say, 'I do love your daughter, but I don't want to get married right now because I was married once before, and it was horrible. It was over fast. I guess I don't want to make a mistake again.' She just stares at me, drinking and smoking for what seems like an eternity. Here is the part I won't forget; she takes the cigarette from her mouth, spews out some smoke and then crumples the butt into the ashtray with so much force, I think the ashtray is going to break." Jeff mimics my mother's face and gesture. "She leans over the table, looks me straight in the eye, enunciating each syllable and says, '*Who- the- fuck- cares*?' Agnes said it just like that. I couldn't believe it. Your mom was the most confident person I've ever met."

My eyes filled and I erupt into joyful laughter, doubling over on my straight-backed chair with my arms across my stomach.

Jeff doesn't understand my reaction. "Why are you laughing?" he asks.

I shake myself into seriousness and get my question out. "What happened then?"

"Well, at first, I was shocked, but then the scotch kicked in. I stared at her, not believing she said that, and then I started talking, telling her about my first marriage, and about all the warning signs I ignored. Then I tell her the real reason—basically, I walked in on my wife and her boyfriend. I never even told my parents that."

When we returned from our vacation, I kept replaying that night and I figured out she was telling me to stop being afraid, and that it *is* time for me to move on. It was. A few months later, you and I got engaged." Jeff grins at me until his chin clef deepens. "She was right. I was stupid."

I take an audible gulp of air, and I realize I have been holding my breath. I stand up, reach over, and grab his chin, bringing it over to mine and I smack kiss him on the lips hard. Still so wrapped up in his story, he asks, "What was that for?"

I don't answer; I will tell him later. My fingers curl over his broad shoulders, "So you knew this all along and you didn't tell me? Why now?"

"I don't know. I guess I was embarrassed. She popped into my head with the wedding and celebrating. Agnes would have loved being here tonight."

"Yes, she would," I agree.

Jeff gets up and crosses the empty dance floor to the bar. I marvel at his story, realizing this is my mother's signature move—finishing unfinished business, tying up tethered ribbons into a bow. As when those who are left behind can summon those who are gone through their stories. Jeff is the one who places the gift of *her* in my hands.

I place my hands on the chair back and shut my eyes. To quiet my stomach, I focus on the errant sounds in the room, relax my extended cheeks, turn inward, and take a low-rooted breath. I feel her next to me as if I had just talked to her, and it surprises me. She has been gone for two years, but tonight she is here. With my next intake, my mother comes back into my body again, finding its old space, the memory filling what was a void with her vigilant caring, her stalwart singularity.

They diagnosed my mother about a month after we got home from Scotland and things moved fast. We did not know how to say those words aloud that should have been said or how to etch our bond into permanence. We just reacted to what was coming without speaking, hung onto every day without thinking about what would change us forever.

From now on, my only choice is to become a vessel to conjure her, to conjure Jeff, and to pass on words about those I loved, who were lost, so they can be found.

***

Darlene Williams began her writing career with a memoir. She was born and raised in Chicago and is a retired secondary school Art and English teacher with a Master of Science in Education from Northern Illinois University. During her teaching career, she designed and taught an Advanced Placement Art History class and a series of Computer Graphics classes. During the pandemic, Darlene began taking writing courses from the Newberry Library and is currently a tutor at Moraine Valley Community College. Darlene enjoys taking care of her home, traveling to exotic places, and walking in the forest preserves of the Southwest side of Chicago.

24 | About a Song from 1980 by Sarah Butkovic

I've been thinking about memories recently, and how funny it is that something we've experienced all our lives can take on a completely new meaning after a poignant encounter. How smelling grandmother's fresh bread every Sunday is something arbitrary until she's no longer around to bake, and now the saccharine smell of freshly gilded brioche at supermarket bakeries summons her memory, whereas before it wouldn't have been a second thought.

It fascinates me that our senses have the power to absorb nostalgia until they're swelling to the brim, begging to burst at the slightest opportunity. Memories act like inflated water balloons whose skin has stretched to translucency when carrying heavy emotion. They explode at the slightest jolt, the faintest scent of yeast from a nearby bakery, so desperate to be remembered.

Songs do this often for me. When I was first introduced to The Buggles' *Video Killed the Radio Star* as a rambunctious preteen, I never imagined its pertinence in my adult life, let alone expected to remember it past a year down the line. It doesn't spark one specific memory, but rather brings back the ghost of the person who introduced it to me: the precocious, explosive, highly intelligent boy who remained a steady crush until age sixteen and was my first love.

Aaron was a family friend who lived in our neighboring state, and due to the extensive distance, I only saw a couple times a year. With our birthdays only a few weeks apart, the two of us literally grew up together, creating an unbreakable solidarity. We frequented each other's summer homes and slept in the same bed during that quicksilver age, when that meant nothing more to us than drifting off in each other's company. We showed each other new curse words we heard on TV and drew goofy faces in the playground sand. I can mark my stages of adolescence by connecting them to a memory of Aaron, and *Video Killed the Radio Star* brings them all back in a randomized blunder of visuals and spatial campfire sparks, tiny stills of bittersweet moments burning into a velvet sky that dissolve into nothing the higher they swirl.

When I was twelve, the two of us snuck up his lake house stairs where his parents slept, wandering through the kitchen, searching the cabinets in a quest for forbidden snacks. It must have been one or two in the morning because the kitchen was abandoned in a way that suggested the night had stolen our parents suddenly, their half-empty cups and grease-stained napkins lying askew on the granite. As we gathered our loot, a small noise from down the hall sent us fleeing to the living room. We quickly removed the cushions of a nearby sofa and crammed ourselves inside, haphazardly pulling them back over us in a desperate attempt to blend into the couch. We listened intently for footsteps, our bodies pressed together like two sides of a peel-back sticker, quickened heartbeats pounding in tandem from the thrill of the chase.

I remember feeling euphoric in that moment, ecstatic to be so close to him. So close that I didn't even need to extend an arm to touch his body. All I had to do was exist, expand, and breathe against and with him. I wanted to stay like that all night. I wanted to hear his lungs sigh with every breath and listen to the steadfast pump of his heart grant another round of life to his body. I wanted him to be the refuge that our pillows had been, but I knew such a silly thought was not worth expressing, and he quickly got up to leave. I watched him put the couch back together and tiptoe downstairs so casually. How I envied him, so naïve to the weight of what had just happened, not even giving it a second thought. And I don't think we ever got our snacks that night.

When I was sixteen, I saw Aaron for the first time in over a year. With both of us in high school and picking up extracurriculars, our parents seldom bothered to manage our teenage schedules to get us together. The only reason I saw Aaron that September was because both of our mothers were dying to attend the same outdoor concert. Everyone was sprawled out on the neatly trimmed park lawn, picnic baskets and beer cans by their side, swaying to the verve of the Big Band music. Glimpsing Aaron's newly matured face and body reposing on the grass that night left me nonplussed. I remember the equal balance of nerves and excitement building up to our reunion suddenly replaced with an emotion so confusing I didn't have a word for it. In the past, I longed for his body in an innocuous way, simply wanting him around me as a friendly companion. Someone to smile and laugh with, to talk and make memories. But now, flushed with the poison of adolescence, I found myself yearning for something different, something new—*his mouth*. I wanted it on me in no specific place at all. I wanted to feel his lips on my skin, to feel a spark between us. I was so caught off guard by this feeling that I felt almost nauseous. If my parents weren't around, I would've taken a swig of their drinks to numb my senses.

Aaron had come out as gay only a few months prior, and the fact that I ached for him so fervently made me feel dirty and selfish, because he was incapable of reciprocating the feeling. I was genuinely happy for him, so why did my hormones have to soil what could've been a blissful evening? I asked myself this unanswerable question for hours on end, body and mind in a persistent duel, the unpleasant mix leaving me chagrined all night. I didn't dare look him in the face in fear of my eyes wandering down to the soft curve of his coral lip perpetually set in a gentle pout. It was nothing short of torture.

Having exchanged little more than small talk and not even offering a hug goodbye, I silently bawled my eyes out in the car ride home and let the briny tears dry on my cheeks as punishment. Their dampness turned into brittle skeletons trickling all the way down to my chin. I had spoken mawkishly and awkwardly all night, too betrayed by my own desires to have a good time with one of my favorite people on the planet. I kept telling myself that I was a fool, a dumb teenager with stupid thoughts and ridiculous emotions. The memory of that day haunted me for years to come, and I hated myself every time it crept into the forefront of my brain.

But this too shall pass, and so it did.

Memories like the ones Aaron and I shared as kids ultimately overshadowed the one from the outdoor concert. I have so many stored away. They're the reason I fell in love, and The Buggles' catchy one-hit-wonder is the key to unlocking every last one. That song strikes a chord deep within me. To be ten, listening to the opening notes for the very first time, their bass pulsating through the radio speaker as we loaded up his mother's CDs, so peppy and vivaciously carefree. To be ten and fall in love all over again, I would trade the world for every cent and every dollar to my name, as long as I could still experience all the memories yet to come.

I hear that song and I think of it all. The ungodly hours spent on *Animal Crossing*, torpid nights of board games and cards, directing homemade movies on a prehistoric camera, all while *Video Killed the Radio Star* resounds in the background as a track to great memories of my life. I hear it and I think of everything. I hear it and recall him.

***

Sarah Butkovic received her BA in English from Dominican University and received her MA in English from Loyola University Chicago. As a writer, she has published creative and journalistic work within and outside academia, including a news piece in a local Chicago paper.

Although she dabbles in other genres like creative nonfiction and poetry, she has a soft spot for gothic fiction and specifically short stories. Ray Bradbury is her most frequent literary muse, as well as her favorite author. She reads *The Halloween Tree* every Halloween.

Sarah is currently an editorial producer for Simpler Media Group.

25 | Portal Magic by Janet Pfeffer

My mother and I stand at my father's grave under an austere blue sky. It is February; the air is crisp, the clouds display faint veils of softness. This is our first visit since my father passed eight months earlier. We are here to select a gravestone for his unveiling. Apparently, there are savings in purchasing one stone for both my parents, a fact my mother and I light-heartedly agree my father would appreciate. He loved a good bargain. For a moment, it almost seems sweet to mark their time partnered together on earth with a shared stone. *Almost.*

Positioned between their resting places, this double stone would be fully inscribed on the left:

Paul Weissman
November 13, 1929 – July 9, 2019

On the right, only a dash would follow my mother's date of birth.

Leila Weissman
January 17, 1932 –

Nestled between our defined beginnings and our elusive vanishing points, this dash exists for all of us. Yet, the idea of a dash engraved into stone, waiting for my mother in the ground, horrifies me. We order a single stone.

It's been only one month since my father's passing and my mother is preparing for her death. *Morticia*, she calls herself when working on this project.

"I think I've finished the guest list," Morticia says as I arrive. Standing in her kitchen, she warms the delicious quiche she has prepared for us. Despite her petite stature, she is tall in her presence.

After lunch, we sit down on her bed as she pulls out memories. She has already begun giving her things away, a gentle obsession she has indulged in since my father's passing to make it easier for my siblings and me. At eighty-eight and a half, Morticia has peeked over the horizon.

One by one, we open small white boxes of jewelry that she has accumulated as a young woman and over sixty years of marriage to my father, who loved to buy her things.

"I finally told him I don't have enough necks," she said smiling.

There were treasures from every era of her life. Among her precious objects is the remnant of a high school graduation present. The face of a watch she had been given, now absent from its band, repurposed as a pin. It bears a delicate face, far smaller than anything I would imagine wearing, and yet it is my favorite. It offers magical transport to her graduation from Hunter High School in 1949, a place I always thought she had planned to go.

"I actually wanted to go to Taft High School," she tells me.

"Do you want to be the smartest of all the dummies?" my mother recalls my grandmother asking her.

She explains, "It was co-ed, and I was boy crazy. Taft didn't have the reputation that Hunter had, and Grandma wanted me to be able to support myself. She wanted more for me."

For a moment, my mother is lost in thought, as if replaying her mother's words.

"That was one of the best decisions of my life," she said. "I learned there was almost nothing women couldn't do."

The memories of her life seem to float just above us that day, at times landing.

"Your father was the love of my life," she says, "but not my first love. There was also Lefty and Harold." I have heard of both of them, but for the moment, I am focused on being my father's daughter.

"Did you love Daddy most of all?" I ask her in a manner so childlike that as the words leave my lips, I am already smiling at myself.

"Differently," she said. "He was smart, handsome... funny. And I thought he would make a good father."

In my father's last year of life as his dementia progressed, I returned to playing guitar after a lapse of forty years. I was never particularly good; it had been my older sister's instrument, but I saw an opportunity. Week after week, I would visit my parents with my recently purchased guitar. I created a new ritual with my father, rediscovering the music I played as a teenager. My dad, seated on his favorite cozy swivel chair, listened as I sang *Take Me Home, Country Roads* to him. Hands clapping, he always chimed in for the chorus.

I understood music would be our last language. I sang those words to him like a prayer to ease him gently and lovingly home. As our song joyfully filled the space, I could feel his absolute delight in me as he smiled, singing along to the few words he knew.

What I didn't know then was that I created a musical portal. Later, by singing those words, fingers strumming my guitar, I could still feel his loving gaze. Later, I could somehow still be in his essence.

It is April, May, and June. I am visited, almost daily, by cardinals. They appear in my backyard and walk right up to my window. We have owned this house in Florida for fifteen years, but this is the first year of the cardinals. They dart across my vision at the entrance of our front door. They travel in pairs. The male, a bright majestic crimson. They are divine messengers, pointing me to the preciousness of time I have left with my mother. And in those early days of the pandemic, I look for my future portals. How will I keep her with me after she too is gone?

As a child I saw my mother as red and myself as pink. She was strong, smart, and direct. I was smart but diffuse, perhaps even

138

manipulative, bending the rules of the game whenever they confined me. And rather than following in her scholarly footsteps, I charted my own course. Clever, maybe, but I never saw myself as an intellectual. She was an educator, at first a classroom teacher, then a reading teacher, and by the time I was sixteen, an elementary school principal. Deeply engaged in her PhD when my dad had a heart attack, she stopped, not knowing how much time they had left together. He lived another forty years.

"I never regretted giving up my PhD to spend time with Daddy," she told me. "It was the right decision."

One month after my father died, just before Covid, I returned to graduate school to pursue an MFA in creative non-fiction. Enthralled with the subject and the richness of the community, I dove into my studies. I finally became a committed student like my mother, and I invited her to share my experience, read some of the literature, and my own work.

"I never see metaphors," Mom told me after reading some of Virginia Woolf's *To the Lighthouse.*

"You have never been taught to see them," I told her. "Once you start looking, you will." And so Red, with its clarity and strength, and Pink with its poetry and spaciousness, learned together.

I am still in school. My mother Leila is still living in her two-bedroom, spending a lot of her days physically alone. But we are very much together, turning to each other for encouragement, support, and intellectual repartee. We go back and forth, in and out, like the breath. My mother and I discover fuchsia is now our color. It is late one night, and we are chatting on the phone.

"What am I going to do after you're gone?" I ask my mother.

Without hesitation, she says, "you're going to continue to talk to me."

***

Janet Pfeffer is a creative non-fiction writer, poet, and teaching artist with an MFA from Sarah Lawrence College. After breast cancer and a devastating depression, she turned to writing to make sense of her trauma and discovered the magic of storytelling. Her work is a meditation on the creative role of women as writers, mothers, and spiritual beings.

She has been published in *Visible Ink*, Memorial Sloane Kettering Hospital's annual anthology and Sarah Lawrence College's *LUMINA Journal*. Janet recently completed her memoir about healing from cancer and depression, along with a collection of essays and poetry.

In her memoir classes at Mount Sinai Hospital's Dubin Breast Center, Sarah Lawrence College's Writing Institute and The Amagansett Free Library, she teaches writing as a life-changing tool, guiding others to explore their stories and transform their futures.

Janet spends her free time in New York City with her husband, dog Rori, and two young-adult children.

26 | To All the Hood Boys I've Loved by Rogelia Lily Ibarra

For Adam Toledo. May he rest in power.

Junior represents my earliest vision of male brown beauty, with a threatening smile on an elusive pimped up BMX bike, popping a wheelie. Your girlfriend Vane and you watch him longingly from behind the gangway gate. He is distant while you and she are close, so it allows us to discover our preadolescent bodies, peeping and touching. You let her lead. This feels safe and also forbidden.

A new hood, seventh grade, and the elementary school dance: dimmed lights, the lingering tune of a familiar freestyle ballad mixed with acid house...*Fantasy girl, you make my dreams come true...* That's when Lil' Lupe nudges you out of your stupor to hook her up wit that one cute smallish boy and you wing it, fuck it, she's your homie, and her scoring is you scoring. As you walk halfway across the gym, you lose focus in his casual and insecure lean against the cool concrete wall, foreseeing your unintended betrayal of her when he sees you instead. His seduction of you, and yours of him, is subtle and incremental, because he is like a man boy. Short, frail, and pretty, kind of innocent, but he holds deep street wisdom. This encounter unexpectedly jumpstarts your first adolescent romance, which is sealed when Lil' Man asks you to "be his lady" as you both walk his restless Pitbull around the block. Your heart flutters and sinks simultaneously as you know you've also lost your homegirl Lupe's trust forever, because she "saw" him first.

You walk to school together, and before crossing the train tracks, Lil' Man says, "Hold up, babe, dropping something off."

He stops by your other home girl's crib, to see her ma instead.

Ms. Conti hollers, "Y'all are too cute!"

She waves. You are twelve and thirteen. He sells her a dime bag.

Lil' Man remains your "official" middle school boyfriend, yet you don't ever get to introduce him to your parents or get chaperoned to movies. Boys like him might not be welcome in your home, but you're unsure because your parents never have this conversation with you.

Breezy, heavy, drawn-out summers and unpredictable nights. Sitting on stoops, sucking on watery *paletas* as you see the 22's and LA boys promenade with their pressed khaki shorts and oversized jerseys. They're like peacocks flaunting their colors and moving their young bodies to a distant rhythm, familiar and inaccessible. Your reverie is broken as one saunters away from the flock. This older teenager looks your way, calling your name and coaxing your budding puberty. You hold your breath.

The following day, you excitedly slick back your hair into a high ponytail, put on your best mini mall silver hoops and slather the cheap bright cherry lipstick, hoping he'll walk past your building again. You don't want to reveal your new obsession to your girls, Juanis and Lisa, as you choreograph your imagined dance routine to Cynthia's *Change on Me, Your Love...* You want to be loyal to your homegirls' rituals, but the song lyrics tell the developing story in your heart. If you confess, they'll taunt you, saying you're crazy for aiming your love that high. And they're right. Tall High Boy lingers around the hood, but nothing ever comes of this crush because he has a steady girlfriend. You stay confused a while, letting the allure of having an older boyfriend who exudes the popularity and excitement of being a 22 boy[1], yet seems to offer a feminine softness you can't explain or understand yet. You finally confess your curious affection for him to your girl Norma in one of those origami-like letters you love to write with fat cursive, and stick it in your back pocket, forgetting about it when you lend your jeans to her older sister. She finds it, doesn't call you out, but decides to tell her girl, Tall High Boy's lady. They silently ridicule your Icarian desire and secretly laugh whenever you walk past their stoops. Tall High Boy never looks your way after that.

The summer lingers as all the neighborhood kids mix childish and more daring play. Stolen kisses from other random neighborhood boys in the dark during *bote picado*[2] in walkways, in the eclipsed corners of diverging apartment buildings. You run the risk of experimentation with these growing man boys, who show you love and curiosity in their eyes, as they anxiously grope your developing body.

These boys you begin to love never stay. They're too afraid because they sense the growing fire in you. They move to the next girl, slightly older and bustier than you. Like that one who got punched in front of you by that unpredictable angry homeboy, Ruco, you started messing wit. He had you fooled too. Acting like an older brother at first and standing in as the protective security of the hood. But his anger runs deep, perhaps because his father is no longer around. Or he can't handle the constant macho pressure of his homeboys. You could have been his steady girlfriend. But he disappears and then comes back with another girl, and she's pregnant. You snap the fuck out of it when you see him hit her, you cuss him out realizing it could have been you. With fear and relief, you pack in the rage.

---

[1] A gang of mostly Latino boys from the southside of Chicago and Cicero in the 80s and 90s.
[2] Translation: Mexican kick-the-can game

You hear about that other small-framed one, Frankie, the neighborhood Latin lover with the beautiful face, raping some girl from the daytime parties, the ones you skip school for. And you remember that time you gave him a hickey and slipped away before he was able to burn you by holding that hairspray can to your face and setting it on fire with a lighter. First lesson learned about homemade hood weapons! You barely knew him but wonder if his looks and swag help him get away with a lot. A fleeting memory, like the short-lived hookups at these parties. At least that's the expectation, and the sense of belonging if you even get noticed by one of the popular boys, like Frankie. You repress that maddening moment and decide he's still *fine* but an asshole.

Years later you get the *chisme*[3] about ole' boy Chuco getting your other homegirl Lil' Lupe pregnant, and you remember, *chin*[4], she's younger than you and he probably kissed her in the same hallway where he kissed you, as if running out of time. You sense the pangs of fear she must be feeling, especially having to face her strict-ass mother. You pack in the guilt. But you're also comforted it wasn't you who fell for his charm.

Everything comes to a rushing halt when you meet him freshman year. Perhaps the innocent flirtation with violence finally becomes dangerously real. Lil' Lalo has an enveloping smile, bright eyes, and that same discordant dancing walk. He is unique; seems out-of-this-world, almost regal and he knows the whole pinche school and stops to small talk with everyone. Lil' Lalo asks you to be his locker partner and you agree in a confusing instant, thinking he could be your first real high-school boyfriend. He looks at you differently, like you're the only person

---

[3] *Chisme*: "gossip" in Spanish
[4] *Chin*: a euphemism in Spanish for "chingar" that translates to "fudge" or "frig" in English

144

in the hallway during those few encounters. You want more, but sense he belongs to no one. Perhaps nothing would have developed beyond this crush, but you never find out.

Lil' Lalo is stolen from you and the rest of the world in a millisecond. His body is mistaken with the wrong colors, the wrong brown body, or who the hell knows?! He could have been anyone, like the other fallen bodies from the hood, but he seemed to love everyone more deeply despite the fear that surrounded everyone in the neighborhood. That bright-ass spirit. Left simply to remain the pastel-colored, air-brushed name on someone's memorial t-shirt.

Something in you dies forever.

Depressed for months, you don't give a shit about anything, and your mom keeps making excuses to all her church *comadres* and your *tías*, "Oh it's just gastritis," she explains. *Mi pobre niña.* And you play along and drop out of school for the rest of the year.

But for reals, we haven't even talked about the hood boy who haunts all your teenage years. Cisco was like a brother. You loved him like family. Larger-than-fucking-life and the highest-ranking leader of the 26 boys[5], or CEO more fittingly, at least that's how you see it now. The darkest ambiguous skin and deep dimples, folks didn't know where to ethnically and racially categorize him. Perhaps that's why he got the shit beat out of him by local cops all the time. But they too were on his drug *mordida*[6] list. As they say, "Live by the sword, die by the sword." Cisco's story is a familiar one, like all the other

---

[5] A gang of mostly Latino boys from the southside of Chicago and Cicero in the 80s and 90s. They were rivals to the 22 boys aforementioned.

[6] *Mordida* literally translates to "bite" in Spanish, figuratively meaning a bribe.

homeboys you have known. He may have even recruited and mentored some using the laws of the hood.

You have learned as an adult that Cisco embodied the romanticized violence of your youth. The unsung heroes of the hood, with entrepreneurial spirits, fly-ass clothes, too damn smart for school because they learned the laws of the streets and hacked capitalist codes. They bought their pretty Latina girlfriends brand new Mustangs, rented limos, and bought fancy champagne for prom nights. How did we separate the hood security that our brothers, sisters and friends in gangs offered us? Was the hood organizing their brilliantly invented reaction and response to the lack of resources that made our neighborhoods so vulnerable? What was the real violence? Who were the true heroes and the real criminals?

You remember the track suit you wore leaving the hood that marked most of your young life. You were fifteen, but felt different, wiser perhaps, like you were breaking up with all the hood boys you loved. Your immigrant parents simply rented a new apartment in a new neighborhood, no safer, no less divested, or less complicated. You did not look back as you rode the educational track to "success" right out of these hoods to the greener pastures of small college town, USA. Was it your light skin? Were you too nerdy to stand out? Was it the fear your parents instilled in you? All their incessant prayers and churchgoing? Your hard work? Or just plain ole luck? You had many community friends and mentors, family members, and the privileges you carry on your body, that you suspect helped lead you out.

But maybe it was not the hood boys you left behind. Along the way you realized who really failed those abandoned boys ... and hood girls. And somehow, you were the one that got away.

***

Rogelia Lily Ibarra lives outside of Chicago with her two young daughters and husband. She is the daughter of Mexican immigrants, identifies as Latina, and was born and raised in Chicago. Ibarra holds an MA and PhD in Hispanic Languages and Literatures with a concentration in Gender and Women's Studies from Indiana University, Bloomington. For the past eighteen years she has taught, mentored, designed curriculum, and been involved in academic scholarship, community organizing and advocacy.

Ibarra experienced and survived postpartum psychosis after her first child's birth in 2014. This experience created a new journey of awakening, healing, and continued advocacy, such as sharing her life through storytelling, creative non-fiction writing, performance, educational workshops, and community organizing.

Her work covers topics such as toxic masculinity, meritocracy, motherhood, ancestral healing, folklore, mental health awareness and stigmatization. She recently published a micro essay in *Nonwhite and Woman: 131 Micro Essays on Being in the World*, with Woodhall Press, and has a co-authored story in *Chicago Mosaic: Immigration Stories of Objects Left, Lost, or Kept*, with Big Shoulders Books.

Ibarra is currently self-employed and specializes in educational consulting.

27 | My Mother, My Daughter, My Self by Diane Kastiel

I lost my mother when I was fifteen. I don't mean that's when she died, I mean that's when she stopped being my mom. My parents' tortured marriage finally ended, and my mother wanted my three sisters and I to choose sides. When I refused, she chose for me, aligning me forever with my dad–the adulterer, the deserter, the villain in her story.

For a variety of reasons, I couldn't go live with my dad. So I stayed with my mom, but she had little to do with me after that. It was a confusing and devastating loss, but I had school, and school saved me. My friends were there, of course, but more important were the teachers—adults who noticed, encouraged, and even praised me. So I worked hard, got high marks, joined clubs. At school, they considered me a good kid.

But in the winter of my junior year, I got a terrible flu and missed an entire week of school. My friends brought my work home each day, and I kept up with it no matter how lousy I felt. But late Sunday night before my return to school, I realized I forgot to study for a major Spanish test, and tests had to be made up first thing in the morning on your first day back.

I had a panic attack that night. It wasn't just about the grade. It was about letting down my teacher. I didn't know what to do and had nowhere to turn for advice. So I did something I had never done before: I called a friend, found out what was on the test, and made a little cheat sheet.

The next day, I reported to test make-up, picked up my exam, and took a seat. I was so inept at cheating that I forgot to wear pants with pockets and tucked the cheat sheet into the waistband of my culottes. But on the way to the test, it worked its way downward and lodged itself in my underwear. By the time I dug it out, I was such a sweaty, agitated mess that I fumbled it, watching numbly as it floated to the floor and landed in the middle of the aisle. I looked at the proctor. She smiled as if I had presented her with a gift. As she stood up, I looked down, waiting for her to come and take me to the principal's office.

I'd never been in the principal's office before, but I learned the first thing that happens is they call your home. This was before speakerphones, but the principal somehow rigged his intercom speaker to his phone. You didn't just hear the person on the other end; you heard their voice booming out of this giant loudspeaker mounted on the wall, just above your head.

I was terrified and humiliated. From somewhere deep in my psyche, I wished for what every kid wants when they feel scared and alone: their mother.

I got my mother all right. She picked up the phone on the second ring. The principal told her what happened and, for a minute, there was dead silence. Then I heard the voice of my mother over the loudspeaker say, "That's despicable. *She* is just despicable."

But the day came when I was grateful for that experience. Fast forward thirty years, and I'm with my teenage daughter at the local mall. My Mac was acting up, so I headed to an appointment at the Apple store, and she took off to browse the shops. I had just received the news that my warranty would not cover the very expensive problem with my laptop when my phone rang. It was mall security. They arrested my daughter for shoplifting.

I asked to speak to my daughter, and of course, she was a complete mess. In her sobs I heard fear, humiliation–a child crying for its mother. So I told her not to worry, that I'd be right there, that everything would be okay. But that just made her cry harder. Finally, she collected herself and managed to blurt out, "Why are you being so nice to me?"

The answer came so easily, so simply, "Because you're my daughter, and I love you."

Well, now the waterworks really started, and then I burst into tears just as the Apple guy came out of the back room. He took one look at me and said, "Oh my God, lady—we'll totally extend the warranty!"

But the truth is, if I hadn't felt so abandoned by my own mother, I don't know if I would have acted so compassionately towards my daughter that day. We always tell our kids, "I'll love you no matter what." But when they hurt you, when they fail you, when they do things so crazy you can't even believe that is your child, the hardest thing in the world is to act out of love. But I was able to, at least that day, because I knew exactly how my daughter felt, and exactly what she needed. I could be her parent later—to hold her accountable and discipline her. But right then, what she needed was her mom.

"You're my daughter, and I love you," is what I said and when I did, a wound that had lain open for thirty years started to heal. Because I realized: I may not have *had* the mother I always wanted, but I could *be* the mother I always wanted. And, really, it's the same thing.

There's an expression everybody knows: Love hurts. How true it is, and I doubt there's a person on this earth who hasn't felt that particular kind of pain. But let's never forget that healing is, and always will be, what love does best.

***

Diane Kastiel is a writer and storyteller from Chicago, and the producer and host of First Person Live, a monthly storytelling show in the Chicago suburbs. A three-time *Moth StorySLAM* winner, her work has been featured on National Public Radio's Moth Radio Hour and its podcast, and at special events for WBEZ, NPR's Chicago affiliate.

Diane has told stories on stage at Steppenwolf, The Second City, Park West, the Athenaeum, and Lifeline theaters, and legendary Chicago music venues Martyr's and Fitzgerald's. She's also told stories in more unconventional settings, including bookstores, comedy clubs, art galleries, the basement of a tattoo parlor, and homeless shelters.

Committed to building community and compassion through storytelling, Diane has worked with Story Corps and the Kennedy Forum of Illinois to help people with mental health and substance-abuse disorders tell their stories, and lead the team that developed *Rude to Respect*, a story-based public awareness campaign to empower people with stigmatized health conditions.

Diane works with libraries, schools, community centers, and homeless shelters to bring storytelling to a wider audience and leads storytelling workshops at Northwestern University. She is an alumna of The Second City Conservatory, the University of Chicago's Great Books program, and Northwestern University's business school.

28 | Finding My Someone by Margaret Burk

In 1971, I was living in an urban commune. It was a two flat in the Lakeview neighborhood of Chicago. Eight members of a political theatre collective decided to live together: Robin, Jimmy, Mary, Paul, Laurel, Ann, Don, and me. I was twenty-seven and dating around with an eye for settling down.

We were quite a mix: some were just out of high school while others were in our mid-twenties with established careers. Don and I were among the older set. Some were marijuana enthusiasts, but I wasn't one of them. Some loved rules. Some rebelled against them, especially household chores. We were musicians, dramatists, political activists, and community organizers. We all shared a passionate opposition to the Vietnam War and supported women's liberation and civil rights.

The eight of us lived in a house with four bedrooms. We managed this feat by partitioning the dining/living room in the upstairs apartment with hanging curtains to make four more bedrooms. We drew lots to see who would get the private bedrooms with doors. It wasn't my luckiest day; I hung flowery patterned curtains to partition off my space. There were only two communal spaces—the kitchen and the dining/living room on the first floor.

We all juggled jobs and our political theatre work. I waitressed by day. Night times I rehearsed except for date nights. On this night, the doorbell rang. I added a touch of lipstick and a sexy scarf to my blue jeans and tank-top outfit and headed out for a date with Charlie. He couldn't stop talking about himself all night. Charlie–No!

Charlie dropped me off—no kiss in the car. Disappointed, I went into the house, shutting the door behind me, hoping to sit, needing to unwind. I couldn't find a place to sit in the living room because there was crap everywhere. Books, newspapers, sweaters, shoes, dirty dishes littered the furniture and the floor. The only uncluttered place was the back porch. I grabbed a cup of tea and headed out. Don was there. I just wanted to be alone, but he was quiet and peaceful.

Next day, I was all over everyone, "Pick up your stuff."

Don hung a sign in the living room, "Clutter-Free Zone." *Oh, thank God*, I thought, *Don's on the same page. That's right, Don's bedroom is as neat as a pin.*

Friday, date night, the doorbell rang. I added a touch of lipstick and a sexy scarf to my blue jeans and tank-top outfit and headed out for a date with Ozzie. Ozzie looked at other women the whole night. Ozzie–No!

When I got home, the living room was abuzz with talk and laughter. I headed to the kitchen for a cup of tea. Dirty pots filled the sink. Clearly my roommates had been cooking. They cleaned the dishes, plates, and silverware. But the pots and pans towered in a large stack in the sink. With a sigh, I rolled up my sleeves and dug in. Don came in, and without hesitation picked up a dish towel. In a happy mood, we cleaned together.

Next date night, the doorbell rang. I added a touch of lipstick and a sexy scarf to my blue jeans and tank-top outfit and headed out for a date with Joe. I came home early because Joe couldn't keep his hands to himself. The house was vibrating with music, a strobe light flashing. I jumped into dancing to Aretha, Marvin Gaye, the Mamas & the Papas. About midnight, I needed a break. Don did too. The nineteen-year-old roommates and their friends could go on all night.

We headed to the back porch. It was a clear October night. We sat on the steps looking up at the moon and found ourselves falling into a new kind of conversation. We shared more deeply, telling the stories about our religious upbringings and spirituality, which were taboo topics in our hyper-political community.

Next date night, Lenny rang the doorbell. I met Lenny at a political rally. He was tall, handsome, smart, and taught at the

University of Chicago. Lenny rang my doorbell more than once. Was he the *one*?

One cold January morning, my cousin called me from central Indiana. My dad had died suddenly of a heart attack. The news devastated me. My dad and I were close. I had to leave immediately. I had to go home and be there. Everyone in the house gathered around to comfort me. Then I heard a voice, "Margaret, I don't want you to drive by yourself. I will drive you there." It was Don.

I grabbed clothes, searched for the one dress I owned, threw them into a backpack, and got into Don's white VW bug. I started to cry and tried to stop.

Don said, "It's okay to cry."

I cried the entire four-hour trip. In my tears, I noted how strong and steady his hands were on the wheel. His slim body in a flannel shirt and bell-bottom jeans was calm as we passed miles and miles of corn, bean, and wheat fields. I saw the concern in his eyes as he glanced over occasionally to see how I was doing. We drove to my childhood home. My sister and aunts looked curiously at this long haired, full bearded man who delivered me to their doorstep. It was a bit awkward, but I could see they were touched by his commitment to drive me.

Don paused before getting back into his VW, "Margaret, you okay?"

I steadied myself, bracing for the days ahead. "Yes, I'll be fine. Lenny is coming to pick me up."

Through all the services, family and friends consoled my sister and me. The same family had consoled us years ago when our mother died. But something was missing. Someone was missing. I wished Don was there.

Two weeks later, Lenny came to pick me up. On the way back to Chicago, I realized the wrong man was driving. I kept thinking of Don and the qualities he showed during the year we lived together; his ease with order and cleanliness, playful silliness, spiritual sensitivity, and consistent devotion to a job well done. I gave Lenny a peck on the cheek and went into our house, past the cluttered living room, through the kitchen with its dirty pots and pans to the back porch. Don was there.

Tearing up, I said, "The funeral was hard. I miss Dad so much." He took me in his arms. I breathed deeply and leaned into his embrace. Don's the *one*!

Within four months, we realized we were in love with one another and wanted to make a life together. We moved out of the commune and got our own apartment. A couple years later, we decided to marry because we wanted to have children. All through our marriage, I have seen the qualities that Don displayed on that drive to Indiana, his many kindnesses and generous fun-loving soul. Our shared political, spiritual, and family values have kept us together. through the rough patches: raising three sons, several career changes, and relationship issues. I keep falling in love with him again and again.

Fifty years later, most mornings start like this, "Coffee's ready," Don calls.

I roll out of bed, head to the kitchen, pour a cup and join him on our tidy sunporch, plants at one end and toys and books for our grandchildren at the other end. We have our favorite chairs, Don's on the right, mine on the left. We chit chat about family and friends and do our fifteen-minute meditation practice. Before we head into the day, we take a moment, look at one another and say, "You are the *one*!"

***

Margaret Burk has been fascinated with story since her first career years ago as an actress and theatre teacher. Today she produces storytelling shows and tells throughout the Chicago area and on the national virtual stage. She says even her twenty-year career in fundraising for arts organizations was largely about telling compelling stories. A good story, well told, can open people's hearts and minds, and move them to action. Margaret is the co-producer of Back Room Stories in Oak Park, Il. Her one-woman show *is Irish Roots, a Storytelling Journey*. Margaret teaches *Sharing Your Legacy* classes to senior adults, believing that our stories are heirlooms–gifts to future generations. Margaret also has a story published in Chicago Storytellers from Stage to Page. www.margaretburk.com.

29 | My Daughter for Life by Christina Pinilla

I became a foster parent when I was thirty-seven years old because I was ready to start a family of my own. My mother passed away when I was thirty-two years old, and I decided on Mother's Day to become a foster parent. I wanted that holiday to mean more to me than just missing my mother. I gave up on dating and finding the right guy. It didn't feel like my life was going to work out for me as I envisioned it with a husband and kids.

I grew up in inner-city Chicago, where gangs and crime flooded our neighborhood. By the time I turned fourteen, I'd been exposed to more crime than most people experience in a lifetime. Our cars and home were constantly burglarized and vandalized. On one occasion, I was home when our house was broken into. Thank God they left when I yelled down to them, thinking it was my dad. At age eleven, I was also sexually assaulted. Throughout my childhood, I battled depression and Post-Traumatic Stress Disorder (PTSD).

As an adult, I gravitated to social work. I wanted to create safety and security for children, like myself, who lived with trauma. Working with youth every day in schools, I wanted to give them a loving home, which they clearly deserved. Because I felt that desire so strongly, fostering made sense to me.

It was Mother's Day 2015 when I first sent an email inquiry to the foster center. It took seven months before I finished all my training, home visits, and received my foster-parent license. Less than two months later (fittingly nine months from that first email inquiry), I was face-to-face with Patty. Patty was the first child my agency wanted to connect with me.

Our first meeting happened after a long interview with the agency. I was under the impression that I wouldn't meet her for a while, but they asked me if I wanted to meet her that day. In my head

I was thinking, *oh shit, this is really happening*. They explained to Patty that I would be her new foster mom after an initial trial period. She was excited and came prepared with questions about my favorite food and my favorite color. She was a beautiful eleven-year-old girl. She had long brown, curly hair and big doe-like eyes that could melt anyone's heart. She was smart, playful, and kind. She was also precocious and thoughtful, as well as tenacious and intelligent.

The trial period included biweekly meetings for one month at the group home. We played games, shared a headset as we listened to music on her iPod, and had dance parties while supervised by the agency to assure we were a good match. After that month, she spent her first weekend overnight with me. This was when my nerves really kicked in. It's one thing to spend a couple of hours under someone else's supervision. It's quite another thing to bring her home to stay. But everything went perfectly. We quickly fell into a rhythm of two people who had known each other for years. I took her to see Matilda the Musical and took our first selfie, which shows both our smiles, big and happy, like a couple who had newly fallen in love. We were excited for this new beginning. After a month and a half, Patty moved in. As I brought her belongings into her room, I promised her that we could go shopping for sheets and a comforter that she could choose. And I told her we could redecorate the room however she wanted. I wanted her to feel as though it was her room, her home, her family.

When my agency asked if I was interested in potential permanency with Patty, I said yes, without hesitation. I was longing to be a mother. And Patty was the perfect match for me. We had so much in common, and she reminded me of myself as a child. She was everything I could have dreamed of in a daughter.

But, like me as a child, Patty was traumatized. She had been removed from an abusive home, then moved from her aunt's home to a residential house, and then she came to me. I connected with

Patty's longing to feel safe. And I wanted to give her a loving and safe home.

I apologize to all parents for the naivety of what I am about to say, but I never realized how hard parenting would be. We fought constantly. She would yell at me, and I would yell at her to stop yelling at me. I did not know how to love and comfort her.

One night, after she was supposed to be in bed, we fought about her going to bed on time. She began to pack all of her things. She screamed that she wanted me to call the caseworker to pick her up, "You don't want me! No one wants me!"

I knelt down on her bedroom floor where she was packing and swept my arms around her, slowly rocking her and whispering, "I do want you. I love you. I do want you. I love you. I do want you. I love you."

As I held her tightly and cradled her, something came over me and I wondered if I was comforting her or me. Was this comforting for all the pain she had gone through or for all my past pain? Somehow our two broken souls found each other. When she finally calmed down, she threw her arms around my neck and squeezed so tight I almost lost my breath.

She laid back on her bed and said, "I love you, Mommy."

It took me six months, but I finally received what I wanted. I breathed a sigh of relief. I was officially her mother, and in that moment, I knew how to comfort her in a way only a mother would. Through that experience, I reached a part of me that had been closed off. She was my eleven-year-old self, and I was loving both of us back to life.

We had many beautiful moments together. She took her first airplane ride with me on a trip to meet my family. I remember how scared she was on that flight as we flew to California and how she visited the cockpit. We went to Disneyland, and I'll always remember her shyness when she came face-to-face with the Disney Princesses. Even after all she had been through, she was still a child in awe of Disney Princesses. She called my dad "Grandpa," causing him to swell with tears. And my brother was her "Tío." She even bought him a "Best Uncle" mug.

On a couple of occasions, I surprised her with concert tickets to see her favorite bands. I still remember her messy tears in the backseat of the car when we pulled into the lot at the B96 Summer Bash concert. She thought we were going to church. And there were late nights in a fort we constructed under the dining room table doing our nails, eating Subway sandwiches, and watching silly YouTube videos. On Mother's Day, I took her for her first official manicure and pedicure. Some of my fondest memories with her included the amazing dance parties we had at home where we bonded over our love of dance.

When Patty first moved in with me, her biological family seemed to have no interest in having her back. However, as time went on, they reengaged. And I worried that my new family would not be permanent.

After seven months together, Patty's birth family wanted her back permanently and they performed the necessary steps for reunification.

But she had become *my* daughter. And I wasn't ready to let her go.

On our last day together, I dropped her off at school and kissed her on the forehead, just like I did every day. But on this day, her aunt would pick her up after school. Her aunt would now be her mother, not me. We had eight months together as mother and daughter.

I loved her more than I ever thought possible to love another person.

Through my love for Patty, I faced my repressed traumas. Because of her, I was able to heal myself. So even though she didn't become my daughter permanently, she gave me a tremendous gift.

The irony is that I spent most of my adult life trying to help others and fix their pain, without fully realizing I never healed my own.

I never saw Patty after that last day with her. Though I did try.

A week after Patty left, I met Jerry. With a newly open and patient heart, I was in a better space to date. Jerry and I dated for several years before marrying. Now we have a son of our own.

But I will always think of Patty as my first child.

Today I glanced at the calendar and saw it's Patty's eighteenth birthday. It's been seven years since she was with me. I imagine her somewhere driving a car or wrapped in a man's arms. Maybe she has a job or maybe she's throwing her book bag over her shoulder to head off to a college course somewhere.

I dream of walking on a street and recognizing those doe-like brown eyes.

***

Christina Pinilla is a writer and storyteller in Chicago. She has been featured on SoulPancake, a YouTube channel that tackles the universality of the human experience and she's performed at Mortified, Story Sessions, This Much is True, The Green Mill, and Do Not Submit.

Christina is a Licensed Clinical Social Worker and School Social Worker with Chicago Public Schools. She received a bachelor's degree in Psychology and Theatre Arts from the University of Notre Dame and a Master's in Social Work Degree from the University of Illinois at Urbana-Champaign. She has devoted her life to blending her skills to understand the human spirit and help others by sharing her vulnerable life experiences.

She lives with her incredibly patient husband and her adorable three-year-old on the northwest side of Chicago.

30 | What I Have Forgotten by Millie Ford

I have forgotten the touch of a man, the solid back to hold in the dark, the feeling of arms wrapped around me, coarse wiry hair so different than my blonde peach fuzz. I have forgotten what it feels like to be desired, a coy smile across the room, hot breath on my neck, teeth on my earlobe. I have forgotten the smell of a man, his elements lingering in the air as he walks past, and his taste of salt and history.

I have forgotten the tallness of a man, how an arm can rise like a helium balloon to the top shelf without strain, the big hands turning the lid on the earth, the raw power that propels a javelin or a promise. I have forgotten these memories of you, but they work their way out of my skin like quills. Everywhere I go, I am sharp, something gets snagged, and you are there.

I remember the year when you reached the top shelf to get the casserole dish and made holiday potatoes on Christmas Eve, how the house was transformed with twinkling lights. In our own snow globe, we drank eggnog dusted with nutmeg, and we sang carols. I was off-key; I am always off-key.

I have forgotten how a man reveals himself in small moments, but I remember the water and aspirin brought to my bedside, tequila still resting heavily on my head. I remember the early Sunday morning in spring when you lined up four cars like a bridal procession, wrapped them in soap, water, and wax. You took extra care to clean the inside, vacuumed up the crumbs, and wiped down the coffee spills. I remember you said, "A car is not a restaurant," knowing on Monday, I would take my bagel and coffee to go, and you would love me anyway.

I remember the hair on your chest, your muscular legs, your big feet. My icy toes sweep the bed for you, but you're not there. I remember the simple joys of going out for pancakes, the way your hand reached for the syrup. When our eyes met, you said, "What?" I just shook my head, looked down at my plate. I could never express the depth of my feelings for you in that moment, smelling of maple and butter and bacon. That day, we met your friends and rode motorcycles to St. Charles. You were so proud of me, your bookish nerd, and you introduced me as your girlfriend. You didn't see me as out of place in a biker bar, drinking diet Coke, because I was with you.

I have forgotten what it's like for someone to encourage me, believe I'm brilliant, make space for me. You never stood behind me, tapping an impatient foot, like I did when the football game went on forever. I didn't care except you wanted me to sit with you and pay attention. How can five minutes on the clock last for forty-five? When you laughed at my frustration, your eyes were full of devotion. Now the silence stretches over my Sundays like cling wrap.

I have forgotten the work you did to build a garden for me, bags of soil spread at my feet. That summer, we shared our secrets and fears. You watered. I weeded. We planted a clematis, and we watched it weave around the chain link fence. We hoped for a wall of bright purple, the centerpiece of the yard. I don't live there anymore; does the plant?

I remember the taste of bourbon on your lips when we went dancing on my birthday. I remember the picture someone took. You wore a black silk shirt, and my smile was as wide as a highway because it was the best birthday I ever had. I have forgotten the birthdays and the smiles.

I remember what it's like to be the string on someone's finger, the reminder of connection, the sweet whisper when you would call just to hear my voice. I remember the light on your face when I came home from work. You were in the kitchen making dinner, saying I needed to eat more than cheese and crackers. I remember what it's like when someone empties my pockets before doing the laundry, when dried Kleenex doesn't litter my black mourning clothes, how my socks were all matched, and none were left alone in the bottom of the laundry basket waiting for their mate.

I have forgotten what it's like to have a partner. Now I lug the trash to the curb, drag the stepstool to reach the top shelf, try to breathe in my perfect capabilities. I can do anything, almost.

I remember the trip we made to Lake Geneva in February to see the ice sculptures. Our breath combining to make a wish to the frozen gods. We drank hot chocolate with the peppermint schnapps you added from the flask you carried in your pocket. You were always prepared. You drew me in when a gust of wind blew and snowflakes swirled around the intricate crevices of sculptures, all polished and gleaming.

I remember the blocks of ice the artists transformed with chisels and chain saws to create dragons, mermaids, and swans who mate for life, their necks wrapped around each other for eternity, or at least until the weather changes.

I remembered those sculptures when you died, when a block of ice fell on me, trapped me in three-hundred pounds of nothingness. I had no tools, and my fingers were useless as I tried to claw through the transformed water. I was immobile, a cartoon of who I used to be. I looked through the ice and saw vague forms speeding past. Are people looking at me? They expect greatness; they wait for the shroud of grief to be lifted, for my sculpture to emerge whole.

"A work in progress," said the ice artist. And the people could not wait, they turned, and went home.

I think about what life can look like now, movement and yearning. I think about what it would be like to be warm.

***

Millie Ford earned a master's degree in advertising from Medill's School of Journalism at Northwestern University. She returned to writing after a successful career in integrated retail marketing. Her writing is known for its unique imagery and powerful metaphors. She is currently working on a series of essays she hopes can become a memoir. In addition to writing, Millie is passionate about animal rescue. She volunteers at a local animal shelter to help stray animals get adopted into loving homes. Millie lives in the Chicagoland area with her rescue cat, Isaac. One of her stories will be published in an anthology by LifeStory Publishing in 2023.

About the Editor | Anne E Beall, PhD

Anne is an award-winning author whose books have been featured in *People Magazine, Chicago Tribune, Toronto Sun, Hers Magazine, Ms. Career Girl,* and she's been interviewed by NBC, NPR, and WGN. Her book, *Cinderella Didn't Live Happily Ever After: The Hidden Messages in Fairy Tales* won a Gold award from Literary Titan. And her *Heartfelt Connections* book was named one of the top 100 Notable Indie books in 2016 by *Shelf Unbound.* She received her PhD in social psychology from Yale University and is the founder of the strategic market-research firm, Beall Research.

About the Editor | Judi Lee Goshen

Judi is a writer, actor, and storyteller. Her book *Fornicationally Challenged: My Reluctant Return to Dating*, received a Readers' Favorite Award as well as one of the Top 100 Notable Books by *Shelf Unbound*. She also co-edited *Chicago Storytellers from Stage to Page*, and *True Stories About Love, Vol 1*. She has been published in *Beyond Words Literary Magazine*, *The South Loop Review*, and *Story Salon*. Several of her screenplays and teleplays have garnered recognition from Writer's Digest and The Slamdance Competitions.

As a Moth winning storyteller, Judi has written and told hundreds of stories including her comedic one-woman show: *Fornicationally Challenged*, which was directed by Mark Travis.

Her free time, and her heart, belong to her two grandchildren.

Acknowledgements

This book would not be possible without the talented collection of storytellers who submitted their stories. These authors make this book funny, heartwarming, and meaningful. It was a pleasure to work with all of you. We are grateful that you have shared a part of yourself through your story: Ellen Birkett Morris, Ellen Blum Barish, Margaret Burk, Sarah Butkovic, Claude Clayton Smith, Mary Daurio, Mary Dean Cason, Brie Deyton, Sandra Hager Eliason, Sean Ewert, Nadia Felecan, Millie Ford, Jaclyn Hamer, Dwayne A. Harris, Beth Holly, Rogelia Lily Ibarra, L.B. Johnson, Mark Johnston, Mary Christine Kane, Diane Kastiel, Deborah Kent, Kate MacLauchlan, Dian Parker, Janet Pfeffer Christina Pinilla, Michael Quinn, Emily Rich, Tania Richard, Darlene Williams, and Christine Wopat. You have created a wonderful volume that delves into love in its many forms.

We also want to thank the talented Atiq Ahmed who created the cover for this book. Your design captured the feeling many of us have when we feel loved.

And thank you, reader, for picking up this volume.

Thank you and Feedback

Dear Reader,

Thank you so much for spending your time reading this book. We hope that you enjoyed these stories and found the tellers inspiring.

If you have feedback about the book, you can email us at ChicagoStoryPress@gmail.com. Whether you loved it or hated it, tell us what you think.

Finally, if you have a few minutes, it will help tremendously if you would write a quick review on Amazon.

Reviews make an enormous difference, and the more reviews a book receives, the more people will learn about it.

Thanks again,

Anne E. Beall & Judi Lee Goshen

Made in the USA
Monee, IL
25 March 2023

30530633R00100